The Journey of a Ragamuffin

The Journey of a Ragamuffin

The Pathway to Truth

Bob Head

Copyright © 2021 by Robert F. Head

All rights reserved. No part of this book may be reproduced or transmitted in any form or by any means, electronic or mechanical, including photocopying or recording, or by any information storage and retrieval system, without permission in writing from the author or his assigns.

All Scripture quotations, unless otherwise indicated, are taken from the **THE HOLY BIBLE, NEW INTERNATIONAL VERSION®, NIV® Copyright © 1973, 1978, 1984, 2011 by Biblica, Inc.® Used by permission. All rights reserved worldwide.**

Cover Design and photos by Bob Head

ISBN 978-1-7377704-0-4

Printed in the United States of America

To Joy, Your love for me opened my eyes and heart to God's unconditional love. THANK YOU!

CONTENTS

Acknowledgments 9

Introduction 11

Part 1: Life in the Basement 16

One: The War 17

Two: The Story Begins 21

Three: The Confusion Begins. 31

Four: The Castle 40

Five: Little Boozie 48

Six: Moving On 57

Seven: Shattered Dreams 67

Eight: The Confrontation 79

Nine: Sitting in the Hot Seat 88

Part 2: Lessons From the Basement 99

Ten: The Iceberg That Helped Save My Life 100

Eleven: A Night on the Lake 113

Twelve: Stepping off the Cliff 122

Thirteen: All About Change 130

Fourteen: The Well Worn Path 140

Fifteen: Guitar Lessons 146

Sixteen: The Sinking Boat 151

Seventeen: The Calling 158

Words of Joy (Literally) 169

Jenny's Words 174

Suggested Resources 177

Acknowledgements

I had no idea what I was getting into when I first picked up a pen and began to write. I was also clueless as to how many people it would take to follow this project to completion.

To the One who has guided me through life even when I wasn't aware. Thank you for putting so many people in my life to help direct the path You have set before me. This book being one of them. I am without words to express how grateful I am for Your love for me. Thank You for inviting me to write one more tiny part of Your wonderful story.

To my beautiful and patient wife, Joy. Thank you for encouraging me and giving me the space and time to put these words on paper. You have always been there supporting me in every way. I love you and I love being a team in this crazy world.

Thank you Jenny McCoy, my amazing daughter, for proofreading my manuscript and making it readable so my editors wouldn't have nightmares trying to understand my writing. I am so proud of you.

Thanks to my best friend Joe Donaldson for reading my book and making sure my theology was aligned to God's word. That is of greatest importance to me. Thanks also for the many years of lunches where our conversations helped me to understand a lot of what is in this book at a level I wouldn't have reached on my own. Even if I did pay for the majority of said lunches.

To Nate Larkin. Your email response to me after reading the manuscript, was that last little nudge I needed to make this book a reality. It was especially nice I received your email while Joy and I were celebrating our 40th anniversary in Texas. Your growing friendship means the world to me.

To Jacqui Weishaar and Anna Havrilesko from Polished Editing Services. You guys are amazing. You didn't just edit my book (which you completed with great care), you brought amazing insights to my own book that literally brought me to tears. Being a rookie author you helped me prepare my book for publishing as well. Can't wait to partner on another project.

Introduction

As I have reflected back on life and the things I have accomplished, the realization has come to me that most of those accomplishments occurred because of someone else's intervention or prodding. I have always been envious of the friends I grew up with who knew by high school exactly what they wanted to pursue in life. I have not chosen much in my life. Instead, it has chosen me.

My first job happened because my parents knew I would need money for college. So, they found me a job at a service station. When a decorator who was a friend of a friend of Mom's saw some furniture I had made, she had the owner of a millwork company call and offer me a job. My career in air traffic happened because a coworker at the mill encouraged me to take the initial test, which resulted in my 25-year career with the Federal Aviation Administration. Moreover, my woodworking company came about because people began purchasing furniture I had made for our home. I did not set out to do any of this; it just happened because of prodding from someone else.

Writing this book is no different. I am not an author. Reading has always been something that has inspired me in many ways, but mastering the structure of a sentence is not one of them. At 63 years of age, I still struggle with the English language. It is as far out of my wheelhouse as anything I have ever attempted. As I was researching how to write a book and trying to learn everything I could to write something of value, I came across an article that listed several steps involved in putting a book together. The very first step was to answer the question, "Why do you want to write a book?" The article claimed that answering this question was the first step in being able to complete a successful book.

Pondering the question and the suggestions the article gave as possible "whys," I quickly came up with a few reasons I wanted to write a book, only one of which made their list. Not sure if that is a good thing or not; time will tell. My number one reason for writing is that I was told to. You might as well know up front this is a book about God and one of His sons. God had been prodding me to write this book for many years. People He put in my life had been encouraging me to write for some time — people who knew I was not an author but thought there was a story to be told. His story.

Hebrews 4:12 says, "For the word of God is living and active." While the Bible is a complete book of God's word, I believe He is still writing His story through His sons and daughters today. And He wanted me to write the part of His story that included me. The Book of Bob. It has taken many years to accomplish. In part due to me allowing life to interfere with the process. Plus, I believe there was more life to happen before it was time to start writing.

We all love a success story. So much so, we often write about them too early in the journey. Things sometimes go south, and we need more time for the healing process. Please do not hear me saying that by writing this book I am finished and good to go. The pages to follow will help you understand that is not so. But I did need to get further down the road before I was comfortable with what I would write. In life, there is always room for more growth.

Introduction

Writing this book became part of my healing process, which is my second reason for writing it. For whatever reason, when I reflect on my past and put it down on paper, it helps me to understand and solidify my experiences. There were experiences in my life I had yet to understand, and writing has helped me get clarity.

In the home my wife and I live in, there is a basement. Some areas in the basement contain accumulations of junk that have been part of our lives. We have thrown this junk in piles, not knowing what to do with it. Over time, the piles have continued to grow, and eventually I will need to clean them out. In the process of cleaning, it will take my wife's help to determine the purpose for a particular item and if it is still useful. Some of the collection has been there so long that we do not even remember the story behind why it belongs to us. It will be a painful experience, as there are many memories in those stacks of stuff. Just the sheer drudgery of going back and sorting through it all will be exhausting. Some memories will be happy ones, but others will be difficult. Yet we need to go through the process if we want to move forward with getting our house in order.

This book has been just that for me. I did not realize all that was in the basement of my heart until I began meeting with Chris Wood, who became my counselor. It was a painful but necessary journey. There are still some things in my basement to go through, and I have realized that is part of the process. It will take many seasons to finish cleaning my basement beliefs, even though, like most of us, I would like it done immediately. That is what I believe God calls the sanctification process. However, the journey of cleaning out my "basement" with the help of Chris and God has set me on a path that I never thought possible in my broken state.

The last reason for writing this book is my hope that it will help others who might read it. I know what it is like to live a life of hopelessness. How desperate life becomes and the dark places it can lead to. I want people to know they are not alone. They are loved, and they are valued. My wife Joy and I have the honor of working as marriage mentors through our church. For years, I have worked with and mentored men. One of the comments we hear repeatedly from the folks we meet with is that our story gives them hope for another day. We are quick to remind them that it is really God's story, we are just a small part of it, and He has a story that includes them if they allow it.

I was sitting with a friend of mine this morning listening as he shared the challenges in his marriage and the relationship struggles he and his wife were living with. He shared with me that his wife's counselor recently helped her to see that all of her life, she understood religion and what it was about. She knew her Bible well and had a good handle on what the Christian life should look like. The problem was that she never experienced it. My friend then said, "I think that was a pretty big moment." I excitedly responded, "That is a huge moment! A life-changing moment. A moment I have experienced and wouldn't trade for anything this world has to offer!" This very idea is the subject of the book you are holding.

I, like so many other folks in the church, have lived my life as a Christian, only knowing about God, the Bible, and the Christian journey. We are told about it every Sunday. However, a sermon does not make us experience the journey. It can certainly motivate you to take the next step, but we get to make the choice to take that step. Like a sermon, a book cannot make you experience the Christian walk. I only hope that through this book, you might begin to see the God of

Introduction

creation, the Father who loves you in a way you will never completely understand, and a Father who wants to be in a constant relationship with his beloved in a new light. A light that will encourage you to let go of your fears and dare to be vulnerable, and to reach out to your Heavenly Father and enjoy the life He has in store for you.

Part 1

Life in the Basement

Chapter 1

The War

How did my life end up like this? Where has God been all these years? Is there any hope for someone like me?

These are a few of the questions I asked myself as I sat across from my counselor, Chris. For the next several months, he walked with me as I unraveled the answers to these questions and many more.

Chris would help me understand that while my behaviors were sinful and very inappropriate, the bigger issue was much deeper than the behaviors. And we needed to get to the bigger issue in order for me to be free from the behaviors. At first that made no sense to me. As we kept digging deeper into my life, the knowledge I gained began to take me on a new journey down a very unfamiliar and scary path.

We all have identities that we live by. Some we freely own, and some own us. I would say that most of my life, I had an identity crisis. I did not know I had one, but I did. On the outside, my identity seemed to be very clear to the people around me. Most people would have said that I was a very caring, loving, and easygoing person and a Christian. They would say things like that because that is how I projected my image. That is what they saw. It was a mask I wore. I actually wanted that identity myself, but deep within me, the identity I hid from others was very different and fragile. The other side of my mask was much uglier and troublesome. In truth, I was a scared little boy full of guilt and shame, thinking he was of no value to anyone, especially God. The identity crisis that led me through life would eventually lead me to a crossroad, and I needed help to sift through the pain and experiences that had brought me to this point.

Many do not hit rock bottom because of one particular event. Most of us, including myself, hit rock bottom because of many choices we have made over our lifetime. These choices are a result of lies that we began to believe about ourselves from a very young age. These lies lead us to develop a belief system that motivates our behaviors. Of course, our emotional state is added to the mix.

The challenge this osmosis type of learning brings is the difficulty of discerning when our beliefs actually become an integral part of our lives and the impact that they make. That is, until we hit rock bottom and choose to surrender our old way of life as we dig through the rubble that it has left behind. This is a huge, terrifying choice to make. To leave behind what is known and has worked for us at some level is like sacrificing a comfortable old coat. To choose the new path anyway is leaving the known behind. I would make this choice because it was all I had left. I had run the gamut. I had tried every possible way I knew to fix my broken heart, but to no avail. There was nowhere else to turn. To be honest, I was skeptical about this new path. I had not heard many success stories. What did it matter anyway? I was not worthy of a success story.

Chris helped me to see the war going on inside my heart. A war that had been raging for 40 years. A war that until now I had been content to turn my head and ignore. A lot of life happened during the war that had led me to this crossroads point, and it is best understood by starting at the beginning.

The following is my story. Really, it is God's story of reaching out to one of His beloved, messed up, ragamuffin sons. How He picked his son up out of the filth of this world, brushed him off, cleaned his dirty, tarnished body, and dressed him in a new robe and sandals. How He wrapped His arms around His son, embracing him, as only a loving father can. How He took His son into their home and presented him with a feast. How He told the son how much He loves him and how ecstatic He is that His son chose to come home.

It would be many years before that banquet could take place for me. A lot of life had to happen first.

Reflection Questions

1. Are there behaviors in your life that are keeping you in bondage and from experiencing the fullness of life that God wants for you?

2. Do you wear a mask that hides things about yourself that you don't want others to know? Can you name some of those things?

3. Do you believe God wants to walk with you on a path that will make you more like Him? Why or why not.

Chapter 2

The Story Begins

I remember the day well: It was the summer of 1968, and my family was moving into our new home. The house was actually 40-some years old, but it and the surroundings were new to us. The moving truck arrived, and the movers began unloading our belongings. What an exciting day for us. Everyone seemed to be happy, including myself. My brother Gary and I ran up and down the ramp of the moving van countless times, dodging the movers as they worked. We checked out our small front yard by passing a football back and forth as our older sister Nancye watched.

We spent most of the day outdoors, playing and staying out of the movers' way. They worked very hard filling our home with furniture. 228 South Bayly was our new address, located in the Crescent Hill area of Louisville, Kentucky. A neighborhood where cars parked on the street (in those days, most families only had one), and each side of the street had an alley behind the row of houses. To an 11-year-old boy, this meant an expanded playground. Parked cars along each side of the street became a defensive player during a football game, and the alley became a drag strip for our homebuilt bikes and go-karts. These events came later, after we were moved in and settled.

As we waited — somewhat patiently — outside to see what our new home looked like, and where we would sleep, I noticed an elderly lady sitting on the porch of the house next door to our left. As we continued to play football, my brother kicked the ball over my head, and it landed in the elderly woman's yard. I hesitantly walked toward the ball, fearing the wrath that was likely to come. Instead, I received a cheerful, "Good morning, it sure is nice to have young children moving in next door. My name is Mrs. Wright. What is yours?"

"Bobby."

"Good to meet you, Bobby. I am really enjoying watching you kids playing ball."

"Thank you, ma'am."

It was the first of many conversations that Mrs. Wright and I would have in the years ahead. By conversation, I mean I would listen and respond to her questions that would often go like this: "Bobby, do you know Jesus?"

"No ma'am, not really, I have seen His stations of the cross at our church."

"Do you know that Jesus loves you?"

"I guess so, ma'am."

The Story Begins

"Bobby, never forget that Jesus loves you so much that He died for you so that you may be with Him forever."

"Yes ma'am."

Then, she would bring out cookies and lemonade and read me a story from the Bible. I wish I could tell you how many times this scenario happened, but I will never forget how Mrs. Wright poured into me. She gave me the first Bible I ever owned. It contained the King James Version of the New Testament. In the front of the book, she signed, dated, and wrote this inscription: "This book will keep you from sin, or sin will keep you from this book." Oh, how true this would be in my life. I would not understand this until I was in my 40s, but looking back, I realized that that was the first time I saw God. No, Mrs. Wright was not God, but because of her faith, she allowed God to speak through her. God knew where my life was heading, and He wanted to place His truth in my heart. A truth I would struggle to believe. The truth that Jesus loves me. When I get to Heaven, Mrs. Wright is one of the first people I want to hug and share my story with. That is after Jesus, of course.

The time had come for us to see the inside of our new home. It was a small two-story that seemed huge to me as an 11-year-old. As you walked through the front door, you entered the living room. There was a black and white TV at one end of the room with rabbit ears sitting on top. We would later discover we would have three channels to watch. An old couch and chair also sat in the room.

As you walked through the living room, you entered what would have been the dining room. This room would become my parent's bedroom. It always seemed odd to me that we would walk through their bedroom to eat a meal or leave for school, or when walking downstairs to watch television. Maybe that was wisdom on their part so they could keep track of our whereabouts. Beyond their room to the right was a small kitchen with a round table and chairs. That was the whole downstairs.

Now onto our rooms. The stairway to the upstairs was located in Mom and Dad's bedroom. At the top of the stairs was a door leading to a walk-in closet. Walking past the closet, we came to another door, which led to the only bathroom in the house. All five of us somehow survived life with one bathroom.

Apparently, when the house was built, the idea of showers was not common, and a tub was all we had. Even if we had a shower in the bathroom, I don't think it would have prepared me for what would transpire at school. The first shower of my life took place in junior high school gym class. It was a community shower where each person awkwardly walked in fully exposed and mentally humiliated to find an empty spot. Then the jokes would begin. The jokes were usually focused on the kids with little athletic ability — in my day, they were called "nerds." Being a good athlete kept me from the jokes in the shower, but my last name was Head, and that proved to make me an easy target for humiliation at other times.

Finally, passing the bathroom, we made it to our bedrooms. Gary and I would share the bedroom to the left, and our sister would have her own bedroom next to ours. We thought it was awesome. Our twin bunk beds were waiting for us, along with an old wooden toy box that completed our furnishings. I would sleep on that twin bed all the way through college.

I want to pause here for a moment and remind you that this move took place when I was 11 years old, and what I

The Story Begins

have just shared was the first memory I have of my life. Mom told me that we moved to this house because we had previously rented apartments or houses. This would be the first house my parents owned. It was the first mortgage they were responsible for paying. The first house they could lose. Many families purchased homes back then, but I think this pressure was part of the catalyst that would cause the pain that inflicted our family. Not the only reason of course, but a contributing factor.

In my 40s while in counseling with Chris, we began talking about my childhood, and I shared my first memory of life at age 11. We tried to work back further but to no avail. I came up with two events that different people had told me about, but I did not have any memory of the actual experiences. First, while attending Saint Frances of Rome Catholic School through grade four and while playing outside during recess, I ran into an older boy, fell backward, and busted my head open on the blacktop. Another story passed down was that one day, while being chased by a dog at our old house (which to this day does not look familiar to me), I ran down the street and across the railroad tracks with my mom chasing both of us. Turns out the dog was wagging his tail the whole time looking for someone to play with. I have no experiential memories of these events, only recollections of being told about them.

Chris encouraged me to ask some family members about my earlier life to see if I could understand what may have happened that caused my lack of memory prior to age 11. I did not want to confront my parents about that time. It seemed they already felt bad about our family life after I was 11. Therefore, I asked my older sister who had previously spent an extended time in counseling. When I explained the dilemma to my sister, she commented on how odd it was.

While in counseling herself, she had gone through many processes including hypnotism, trying to reclaim her memory before the age of 15, again with no avail. Ironically, my sister is four years older than me, which means our memories began that same summer moving to our new home. We both agreed that the mystery that erased our earlier memory away would stay unsolved. Do I still wonder? Sure do. Have I moved on? I truly believe I have.

Okay, back to the new home. Our life seemed to be going well at first. I went to a new grade school for the fifth grade, met new friends who lived on our street, and enjoyed many games of football, softball, and foursquare while playing in the street or the field behind one of my friend's home.

I do not know when it happened, probably gradually over time, but somehow my family life changed in a way that would affect how each of us moved forward in life. It began by Dad not coming home at night after work. At times, he would be gone for days with no sign of him. My mom would clearly be distressed, and she became more critical of us, especially when it came to how we had completed our chores. No one knew where Dad was, and Mom would discover he often had not shown up for work.

I began to feel abandoned and uncared for, and things only seemed to get worse from there. At times, he would come home late at night, drunk and mean. I have met many drunks in my life, and it seems they fall into two categories. First, there is the quiet, happy drunk who sits in the corner and has a big smile on his face. The second and more distressing is the mean drunk who is full of anger. My dad was the mean drunk. In my teens, I began developing the potential of becoming a mean drunk just like him. More on that later.

One night in the wee hours of the morning, Dad stumbled into the front door. My mom was a very strong-willed

The Story Begins

woman who would never back down from a good fight. As their confrontation began and became louder, the yelling woke the three of us kids from our upstairs bedrooms. Running to the top of the stairs, we sat down, trying to understand what was going on. The shouting turned into pushing and shoving, which turned into things being thrown, and then the sound of someone falling to the floor. I remember being very fearful, as the three of us held each other's hands. I also remember feeling so helpless at not being able to help my mom. At one point, we all yelled down the steps, pleading with Dad to quit hurting our mother. That seemed to help, as the confrontation subsided, and they told us to go back to bed. In tears, we got up and stumbled back to our rooms to lay back down. It was one of my loneliest moments. I wish I could say this was a one-time event, but it would become more normal for quite some time.

Dad struggled for many years, escaping the challenges of life behind alcohol. Sometimes on weekends, Mom and us kids piled into my aunt's car and traveled up and down Frankfort Avenue. We stopped at various bars along the road and waited in the car while Mom walked in to see if Dad was there. Sometimes she would find him and confront him, trying to convince him to come home. They would stand outside in front of the bar and argue as we watched. Dad would eventually turn around and stumble back into the bar, while Mom walked back to the car, and we returned home without our father.

This took a heavy toll on our family. The three of us became more disconnected from our parents. Mom stayed so busy trying to keep our home intact, and eventually took a job in a doctor's office. That left my sister in charge. Our family needed money desperately. We all had chores to do and were reminded very quickly when they were not done satisfactorily. We stayed away from the house as much as we could. We played in our front yard while Mrs. Wright watched us, or went down the street to play with the other kids.

Something was happening within me at the time as well. I would not understand it for many years. Anger was building inside my heart, and it began manifesting itself in various ways. In fits of anger, I have punched holes in drywall, thrown things at people, and yelled at the top of my lungs.

One winter day, I had been outside playing football and was returning home to warm up. I knocked on the back door to get Gary or Nancye's attention so one of them would come and unlock it for me. Upon arriving, they began staring at me through the glass panels in the door, laughing and taunting me. I yelled at them and told them to open the door, or I was going to throw the football through it. Seconds later, I did.

The football went through the glass, breaking the wood strips that held it in place. We cleaned up the mess and taped some cardboard over the large opening I had created. Cold air flowed through the house. It would not be an easy fix. The three of us sat down together and cried. We knew the trouble that was ahead for us.

Another time, my sister and I began fighting. As we wrestled in our living room, I shoved her against a wall. In doing so, the force of my shove directed her toward an antique guitar someone had given our mom. Her foot went through the body of the guitar, rendering it useless.

Another way my anger would play out was in sports. Even when playing with friends from the neighborhood, I would often get upset and begin a fight with whomever had done me wrong, which sometimes resulted in black eyes and broken wrists. I don't know how I had any friends left who wanted to play.

The Story Begins

I loved playing football at school. In particular, I liked playing defense. I loved the game, but it also gave me an opportunity to release some of my anger in a more formal, appropriate way.

Often, I would think to myself, "Where does this anger come from, and why can I not control it? Will it ever go away?" The anger continued well into my marriage. At times, I could stuff it away and struggle through the day, but it eventually would rear its ugly head.

I think some of my anger was directed toward my family and God. I so wanted my dad to play a bigger role in my life. Things like coming to my football games, helping me build bicycles from the parts we found, or teaching me how to fix the lawnmower someone had given me so I could make some money. I had to do all of these things on my own. And I wish my mom had encouraged me more and been less critical. I know they were facing challenges, but I really needed them to be a positive influence in my life. I was also angry at God. Why would He put me in this situation? I thought He was supposed to take care of me and protect me.

I would eventually learn my anger was rooted in a lie I had begun to believe as a young boy. The lie is that I was not loved and did not deserve to be loved, by anyone on earth or by God. The lie then created a feeling that led to a negative behavior. I was not able to connect the two, and therefore I did not have the ability to overcome my anger for any length of time.

Reflection Questions

1. Have you had someone in your life consistently tell you about Jesus and His love? Do those words resonate in your heart?

2. How has your family of origin helped shape your view of God?

3. How has your view of God impacted your relationship with Him?

Chapter 3

The Confusion Begins

Have you ever looked back and considered past events that had a lasting impact on how you have walked through life? Perhaps you or someone you know said or did something that affected what you believe about yourself, others, and even God.

I believe we can all look back and remember these defining moments that helped set us on a path that we would eventually follow. These moments help develop our identity and the way we live out that identity. This identity is what people will often see in us.

Of course, there are things about ourselves that we choose to keep deeply hidden. Maybe it is being a people pleaser or isolating ourselves from those around us. Maybe it is being a doer at all costs or being a procrastinator. These qualities are not bad in and of themselves, and I believe they are partly how God wired each of us as unique individuals.

Our identities are often created in our subconscious, and we may not understand how they came about for years. And the messages we hear that eventually become truth to us often contradict one another. This causes a constant state of confusion within the deepest parts of who we are. We live in constant struggle with what we say we believe and what we actually believe deep in our hearts. In *The Ragamuffin Gospel: Good News for the Bedraggled, Beat-Up, and Burnt Out*, Brennan Manning states, "The alternative to confronting the truth is always some form of self-destruction." This would be true for my own journey for many years.

At the age of 12, I experienced two such events that have affected my life greatly. They would keep me in a state of confusion as to what I believed about myself for years.

Day after day, I would sit on Mrs. Wright's front porch as she read me stories from the Bible. I came to understand that she had been describing through scripture the way of salvation, and my heart became more and more convicted. To get a deeper understanding of salvation, I began reading the Bible Mrs. Wright had given me. It was a King James Version of the New Testament, and I struggled greatly to grasp the language it used.

I began life in the Catholic faith. I was christened as a baby and celebrated my first Communion. I still have a picture of my first Communion, but I have no recollection of the event. I do not know how often we went to church before moving to our new home. Once at our new home, we occasionally would attend the parish near our previous residence. I remember leaving the church service one time, confused about what the priest was saying since he had spoken in Latin, and I was still struggling with my English.

The Confusion Begins

I also remember going to Confession a few times. I would walk into a dark wooden cubical, close the door behind me, and sit on a wooden bench facing a wall where a priest was waiting on the other side. In the wall was a door that the priest slid open. He then asked what sins I had committed that week and needed to confess. I responded as I guess most 12-year-olds would, confessing when I had been disobedient to my parents, taken toys from my brother, and fought with my sister. The priest responded by providing me a list of things to do so that I could make amends for my sin. The door slid closed, my indication to leave and make room for the next sinner.

It was during this time in my church experience that I began to live out of a works mentality. I began living as if I had to earn forgiveness, acceptance, and love. The idea that if I was going to get anything in life, I had to earn it, became a rule I lived by.

Our church days ended quickly after our move to the new house. My church had become Mrs. Wright's front porch. While I would visit with Mrs. Wright, my sister had met some new friends who had invited her to attend a Christian church in our neighborhood. I began to see a change in her - a softening. We would still have our sibling spouts, but something was clearly changing within her. Maybe it was just having new friends to hang with, or maybe it was something at church. Whatever it was, I liked it and wanted to have the same peace that was a new part of her disposition.

One day while I was struggling reading my Bible, my sister asked me if I would like to go to church with her sometime. She told me about the youth group she was part of, and said she thought I would enjoy going. I had not gotten much from church before, but at the time I was always looking for a way to be absent from our home.

I still remember the first time I walked into the Christian church with my sister. The people seemed to be excited we were there. It seemed much more uplifting then the more somber approach I had experienced at our Catholic church. How much of that had to do with me and where I was in life, I am not sure. When the minister got up to preach, he was also speaking English. Week after week, I continued to soak in what the minister was saying, and his words continued to convict me. I would come home and share with Mrs. Wright what the minister had spoken about, and as we discussed it further, a broad smile would fill her face.

It was during this time that the first of two major events happened that caused great conflict in my life for many years to come. Through Mrs. Wright's sharing of the Gospel and my new church, God had been speaking loudly into my heart. One Sunday, the minister was preaching on salvation. He said that if we believe Jesus died on the cross for our sins and accept Him as our Savior, we would live with Him eternally. After concluding the sermon, he proceeded with the altar call, inviting everyone who wanted Jesus in his or her life to walk forward and be baptized.

I cannot truly say what provoked what I did next. Maybe it was the sermon I had just heard, or the many conversations I had had on Mrs. Wright's front porch. Maybe it was the times I struggled to understand things while reading God's word in my King James New Testament, or the constant tugging I had felt inside my heart. Maybe it was a combination of all these things. I do believe it was God pursuing one of His little boys that He knew was lost and was believing a lot of what Satan had been feeding him.

I got up from the pew I was sitting in and walked forward to meet the preacher. I told him I wanted to accept Christ as my Savior and wanted to be baptized. The next thing I knew,

The Confusion Begins

I was being dunked in a blue baptismal pool with a painted scene of the Jordan River behind me while wearing a white robe. To be honest, I do not remember much more about that day — like whether I was relieved or scared of what my parents would say when I told them. I do not remember any conversation at home about my decision. My mom had grown up in the Catholic Church and my dad in the Christian Church, but I think at that time in our lives, they were both just in survival mode and had no space for religion.

I do remember walking home from church that day, thinking how good life would be from now on. How God would take care of me, and only good things would happen moving forward. Much of this thinking came from what I heard from the pulpit, or at least from what I thought I heard. Some of it was probably just hoping in my heart. As time went on, I also felt a prodding from God calling me into the ministry. How naive I was as a 12-year-old to think that all my problems were over now. The reality was they were just beginning. Somehow John 16:33 had not gotten my attention when Jesus said, "I have told you these things, so that in me you may have peace. In this world, you will have trouble. But take heart! I have overcome the world."

Without even knowing it, that day of trouble was heading my way like a storm coming over a mountain. This and many other troubles would continue throughout my life. They were mostly self-inflicted troubles that were birthed from trying to make sense of the lie I believed: "I am not worthy of being loved."

I was naive about something else, too. I was hearing and reading how God wanted to be a part of my journey and walk with me daily in life. Somehow, I missed or did not take seriously enough that there was also someone who did not want me to succeed in my faith journey. His name is Satan.

Of course, I had heard of the devil, but I always pictured him as this harmless, almost funny character with horns, a long tail, and a pitchfork. Oh how wrong I was, at least about his intentions for me. I have learned that Satan is a liar and murderer. He is "the father of lies," Jesus declared in John 8:44. He is much stronger and more powerful than me at my best. He is much smarter and craftier than I am. He hates God and therefore wants to take me down.

The trouble I have been talking about began when the second big event occurred during my 12th year. I had met some new friends upon moving to our new home and neighborhood. I began to spend time with one boy in particular, as we both enjoyed music. I was trying to learn to play the guitar, and Glenn was well ahead of me. Glenn could not read music, but instead had an incredible ear for it. Whatever instrument you put in front of him, within minutes, he was playing it beautifully. I on the other hand relied solely on reading music to play. My family was not very musical, but my mom loved to sing when she did go to church. She sang at the expense of all those around her. I guess it was a joyful noise though. Glenn and I spent a lot of time at his home, where he taught me how to play guitar. His older brother had a band that played around town, and we would often sit around listening to them practice.

One day, while sitting in his bedroom playing music, Glenn went to his brother's room to find an old electric guitar he wanted me to try out. I had been trying to learn on an old Harmony acoustic guitar that was very difficult to play. The strings were so far from the fret board that they were leaving indentions in my fingers and creating pain in my hands. When Glenn returned from his brother's room, he was holding the electric guitar in one hand and something else in the other. He sat down and told me how to strum an electric

The Confusion Begins

guitar. It was so much easier for me to play. I immediately began to be excited about the guitar again.

After a few minutes of me strumming chords on the guitar, Glenn picked up the other item he had brought in. As he opened the magazine he was holding in his hands, he asked me if I had ever seen a *Playboy*. He handed the magazine to me so that I might peruse its pages. I don't know how to explain exactly what happened within me in those moments of viewing my first pornographic magazine, but I do know there was an immediate attraction for me, much like a magnet has to a piece of metal. An almost uncontrollable excitement went through my body. I experienced a high much as I would experience years later with alcohol and marijuana. Even though I knew viewing this material was wrong, from the first look, I believe the addiction got hold of me. Glenn told me I could take the magazine home, which I did, and that I could trade the magazine for another one when I was finished.

As I write these words, I feel both anger and thankfulness when I think of porn. Anger because of the bondage this addiction would keep me in for much of my life. Anger that because of this sin, I have greatly hurt the people I love most. Anger because it allowed me to objectify God's daughters and completely skew what God's intention of love is meant to be. Anger because the guilt and shame that entered my life through this sin almost provoked me to end my life. Anger even now as I see this sin that Satan uses, causing great havoc in and destroying many marriages around me.

However, I also have thanksgiving in my heart. I am thankful that God used this sin to confront me about a deeper sin I believed about Him. I am thankful that this sin eventually led me to give up all my many feeble attempts to follow God's laws as a way of trying to earn His love. To finally surrender my life and will to Him. In addition, I am thankful that this sin eventually would help me to one day know and experience the God whom I had only read and heard about.

Please do not misunderstand me. I would not encourage someone to follow a path like mine in order to seek God in the most intimate way. Nor do I ever desire to go down that path again. I am just thankful for God's truth as told in Genesis 50:20, when Joseph tells his brothers, "You meant evil against me, but God meant it for good," and in Romans 8:28, when Paul says, "And we know in all things God works for the good of those who love Him." I would eventually grasp how wide, how long, how high, and how deep God's love for me is. I say "eventually" because I would live a lot more life following that day at Glenn's home before these truths became a reality. I would live a lot more of my life believing a lie and living with its consequences.

Reflection Questions

1. What events or interactions in your lifetime impact the path you are on in life today? How so? Were they positive or negative?

2. How has your life changed since you accepted Christ as your Savior, if you have already made that choice? How has this decision affected Satan's attempts at winning you over?

3. Are you embracing the gift of salvation, or are you still trying to earn it? Don't just consider at the intellectual level, but search at the heart level for this answer.

Chapter 4

The Castle

I have never walked through a medieval castle, but I have thought a lot about what it might be like to live in one. For instance, what would it feel like to live inside the thick stone walls? Would it be a depressing existence stuck in a structure with no windows? Would it be lonely? Would you feel safe and protected? At times of war, would you feel secure or concerned that a barricade may be broken through? On the other hand, at times of peace, would you feel safe leaving the protection of the castle? It seems that living in a castle would be a dark, lonely life that would limit one's existence. Not desirable conditions for a home, unless you are driven by fear and the perceived need for protection.

Yet I believe most of us at times have lived in an imaginary castle, which we have built around our hearts. Many times, we build these castles at a young age to protect us from events, people, and other things that have caused us great hurt. In an attempt to escape the dangers of life that wound us, we begin building this fortification as a way to prevent that same pain from occurring again. Sadly, oftentimes these walls are necessary and needed as we grow. The problem is, we lock our hearts inside the castle and become prisoners of what once was a safe haven for us. We lose touch with our own emotions, and the belief system we develop during the building of the castle is sealed tightly somewhere in the deep, thick walls we have constructed. We may not be able to verbalize our belief system, but it does not take long for it to become second nature to us, just as we breathe and blink.

    I have lived much of my life as a prisoner of my own castle. I had built such strong walls that I had no clue who I was or the feelings that lay deep within. I did live in great fear. Fear that if you really knew me, you would hate me. This only built the walls thicker and taller.

    The construction of my castle started as a young boy when I began to doubt that God and the people in my life were able to give me what I needed. I had read in the Bible that God is love, and if I had accepted Christ as my Savior that I became His son. The Bible also says that God loves all of His children. The problem was I had not experienced much love in my life from those around me or from God, or so I thought. I felt like my needs weren't being met, and I didn't understand why. These doubts about being loved were never verbalized to me but were based on my perceptions of how and who I thought should love me. When I didn't feel loved or taken care of, I questioned God rather than my perception, and all of this happened at a subconscious level.

    On the other hand, the porn seemed to help in this area. It was very comforting to me, and in some way, made me feel accepted. I never felt rejected when viewing porn. For a while at least, porn seemed to satisfy or numb the aching I felt in my heart. The problem was that the guilt and shame that followed would take me back to a very dark and empty existence.

Nevertheless, this addiction would continue throughout my life. In times of despair, which were quite often, I would turn to porn to mask my pain and loneliness. Then, the guilt and shame would follow, and I would try harder and harder to quit, only to lapse again to the ever-familiar cycle. At times, I could go months or maybe a year, white knuckling my way through, trying to stop something I knew was horribly wrong.

I do not remember ever purchasing a pornographic magazine, and yet, they always seemed to be around. As a teen, one of my favorite places to hide my magazines was inside an old stereo turntable someone had given me. Once I raised the record platter, there was ample storage inside the cabinet.

When times would be challenging or chaos was rampant in our home, I would run to the stereo cabinet. In the escape that porn provided, I always felt a calming effect inside me. That is, until the guilt and shame kicked in. Porn very quickly distorted my view of women, love, and intimacy. In real life, I would become less interested in the person I dated, and more focused on their appearance and sexual desires.

I was actually very shy when it came to girls and dating. That shyness was probably rooted somewhere in the belief that no one would want me. Toward the end of grade school, girls began to call our home and ask to speak to me. My mom thought it was awful that girls would call a boy. Nevertheless, she tolerated it. The phone conversations were very awkward for me, as I did not know how to relate to girls. It was never modeled for or explained to me. I was much more comfortable communicating with guys, as we played sports or music, or through wrestling and fighting. With guys, there was not always healthy communication, but we did communicate, even if it was in a barbaric sense.

In my younger days, people would tell me that I had the look and demeanor that girls liked. As I write that statement, I realize I can't even define what that means. Often, girls in school would tell me that they liked me or wanted to go out with me. I did not typically pursue girls in junior high or high school out of my awkwardness in communicating and fear of rejection. Even when I knew they wanted to go out with me, I struggled to make the phone call to set up a date. The fear was so overwhelming.

I had my first girlfriend when I was in the fifth grade. It was a very innocent relationship. It began by her calling my home and asking to interview me. That was apparently a thing young girls did back in the day. She asked me questions, like what my favorite color was, who my favorite band was, and what color eyes I had. I never understood the last question, as we would see each other in school every day, and surely, she had seen the color of my eyes. I guess conversation was hard for her also, and at least she was brave enough to take the chance.

We began "going together" and attended school activities, like ball games, plays, and the like. Mom always felt that she wore too much makeup. I thought she was pretty, and without making a conscious choice, the girls I dated would often remind me of many of the women I saw in my magazines. Already, I was comparing reality to the masked, touched-up world I learned from what came out of my stereo cabinet.

I met my second girlfriend Lauren while in junior high school. This relationship was quite different from the relationship I had with my first girlfriend. There were some similarities though, as she pursued the relationship like my first girlfriend. Moreover, she also reminded me of the touched-up images I had seen in my magazines. That is where the similarities ended though.

Lauren was much more experienced in many ways than I was. She had already dated guys who were of high school age, and as a result, she had been more exposed to worldly things that I had only read about in books. Lauren's parents went out of town often, and while they were gone, Lauren would stage parties that involved sex, alcohol, and marijuana.

I believe my definition of love became very distorted during this time. Sex and having fun seemed to be the main ingredients that constituted a loving relationship. As odd as it may sound, my relationship with Lauren was the most stable relationship in my life up until that point. She actually expressed love and concern for me, which I was not receiving anywhere else. So, naturally, I thought this was what a loving relationship should look like — dating a very pretty girl, having sex, and partying.

Then, the breakup occurred. She wanted to start dating one of the high school boys again. I was crushed. Another row of blocks went up around my castle.

I was recently talking with a good friend of mine, explaining this epiphany I was having about how my girlfriends so often reflected the women I would view in my magazines. I did not remember consciously thinking that those were the kind of girls I wanted to date. As I already mentioned, the girls were actually pursuing me. I do not know how to say that without sounding boastful, but it was my reality.

My friend responded with, "You were just part of the flock." I replied, "What do you mean by that?" He explained that the girls I dated were part of the worldly flock. I had bought into the cultural lie that the pictures I had been viewing were what girls should look and act like, and the girls I was dating had bought into the same lie. We both bought into a lie that led us down the paths we were walking. The problem was we were following the wrong shepherd, and we also did not have the right people in our lives who would challenge our choices and lead us to the right shepherd.

Yes, my mom would challenge me on some things, and Mrs. Wright would continue to speak truth into me. However, I did not have men in my life mentoring me toward the good shepherd. Without the guidance of men like these, my life would continue to spiral downward. In high school, the spiral escalated. There is no guarantee that having spiritual mentors in my life would have kept me from straying as far as I did, but I do believe my life would have looked different.

There is an old legend sometimes attributed to the Cherokee people called *The Story of the Two Wolves* that illustrates our challenge between good and evil thinking. It goes like this:

An old Cherokee is teaching his grandson about life. "A fight is going on inside me," he said to the boy.

"It is a terrible fight and it is between two wolves. One is evil — he is anger, envy, sorrow, regret, greed, arrogance, self-pity, guilt, resentment, inferiority, lies, false pride, superiority, and ego."

He continued, "The other is good — he is joy, peace, love, hope, serenity, humility, kindness, benevolence, empathy, generosity, truth, compassion, and faith. The same fight is going on inside you — and inside every other person, too."

The grandson thought about it for a minute and then asked his grandfather, "Which wolf will win?"

The old Cherokee simply replied, "The one you feed."

Without even recognizing it, I was feeding the wrong wolf, and all his characteristics were becoming mine. To be honest, I did not even realize I had made a choice.

Reflection Questions

1. What does your castle look like? Do you remember why you needed the protection of a castle?

2. What relationships or situations encourage you to stand firm inside your castle? Why?

3. Reflecting on the Cherokee Indian story, which wolf are you currently feeding?

Chapter 5

Little Boozie

By high school, my castle had been well constructed and fortified. No one was getting in, and somewhere deep within its thick walls was a prisoner named Bob Head. The Bob Head that God created. I was well on my way to creating the new and improved Bob. He was not going to be hurt anymore.

By this time, I believed the sexual experience is what constituted love, and not the person I was with. In essence, the act became more important than the person. After Lauren broke up with me, I closed my heart to the world because I could not survive another heartbreak.

In high school, my life became even more conflicted. At times, I would be very involved in church, and other times, I would be very involved in partying. They rarely occurred during the same period. Looking back, the two scenes were mostly dictated by whom I was dating at the time. As high school continued, the party scene would eventually win over.

This conflict did not stop me from dating. It actually encouraged it more. Without the debilitating fear of losing what I had sealed in my castle walls, I could focus on what I could get from the relationship. In reality of course, the fear never went away, but my ability to mask it greatly improved.

I would at times date girls that would bring me back to church. The "church girls" I dated would often confuse me. At times, they could behave just like the party girls I dated, but they, like me, seemed to be living conflicting lives. We could be singing and playing our guitars, leading a worship service, and hours later, we would be making out in the park. I would be convicted of God's amazing love while sitting in church, and a few hours later, I would be trying to experience my kind of love on someone's front porch.

At the age of 14, I began working at a service station, where we would refuel automobiles and repair them mechanically. I began as a "pump jockey" waiting on gas customers. The job required me to refuel customers' vehicles while checking their engine oil and the air in their tires, and cleaning the windshields. That was standard service in the 1970s. As time went by, Earl, the owner, began to have me change oil in customers' cars and taught me how to carry out other mechanical repairs. Before long, I spent most of my time in the shop working on cars. I would do repairs like brake jobs and tune-ups. Earl would have to test drive the vehicles after I had completed the maintenance because I was not old enough to have a driver's license.

During the school year, I would get to the station as soon as school let out and work until 9 p.m. when I closed the doors. On Saturdays, I would work from 8 a.m. to 6 p.m. A normal workweek in the service station business would be six 10-hour days or 60 hours a week. In the summer, this would be my schedule. As an underage young man, I would get a paycheck for 40 hours and then receive cash for the remaining 20 hours.

I learned many positive attributes while working at the service station, a trade and skill that would help me all through life. It exposed me to many people in a business setting, which taught me a lot about the nature of people and personalities. I learned a great deal about finances and the value of saving that continues to pay dividends in my life. In addition, I learned about work ethic and the benefits of hard work.

However, there were also negative traits that I picked up while working at the service station. The long hours themselves allowed me to hide from the chaos of my life at home. This trait of being a workaholic would follow me well into my adult life in which I would have two successful careers simultaneously. Not because we needed the money, but because it was a way to hide from my perceived belief that my family at home did not care about me.

Another negative trait I gained while at the service station was the opportunity to practice the performance-driven lifestyle I had learned while attending confession at church. I became a people pleaser. As I accomplished good things at work, the accolades from Earl and our customers gave me a sense of acceptance. In turn, I wanted to work even harder so I would receive more accolades. This became another way I strived for love and acceptance.

For any of you who can relate to people pleasing, you probably know what comes next. Exhaustion. Resentment. Fear. Anger. It is very exhausting when you always have to be "on," always working for the next "trick." It didn't matter how successful I was the day before — that love and acceptance would disappear, and I needed to feel it all over again. Sounds a little like an addict's behavior, don't you think? Of course, resentment followed, because now I knew I had to work hard again. I wished someone would just accept me for who I was. No performance. No jumping through hoops to earn something. Just me.

As a people pleaser, I lived in a constant fear of failure. What if I was late for work? What if I could not fix a car? What if people did not like what I said, or what I looked like, or that I was poor? What if they did not like me after I had done everything possible that they asked of me? What if...I wish I knew how many times those words played out in my little head.

Living with a fear of failure was followed by a deep sense of anger. Anger at myself for where I was in life. Anger at the people in my life who were supposed to love me and were nowhere to be found. Anger at all the people who wanted a piece of me to help them accomplish something they needed. Moreover, anger at God because He put me in difficult circumstances and then left me all alone.

Then there were the other things that I learned at the service station. Being the youngest employee, I was surrounded by some very experienced individuals eager to share their worldly wisdom. Such as how to get ice cold beer by spraying a six pack with a Freon tank, how to power shift during a drag race down Frankfort Avenue, how to make out with girls behind the service station, and how to know when girls were flirting with me while I was repairing their cars. I was encouraged in so many wrong ways that it allowed me to lead a very confused life.

We worked on many of the cars belonging to the seminary students who attended The Southern Baptist Theological Seminary, as it was close to the station. One of the seminary couples who had been customers for a few years had recently divorced. They both continued to come to the station individually. One busy afternoon, the ex-wife came to the station because her car was leaking antifreeze. I did not have time to repair it, so I asked her to come back in the early evening. She returned that evening for me to replace her radiator hose, wearing revealing clothes. After repairing her car, she wanted to take me to dinner to "thank me." After dinner, she invited me to her apartment for a drink, where she tried to seduce me. As a high school student, this whole experience did not make much sense to me, and I politely excused myself. I wanted to focus on girls my own age.

I could write a whole book about my experiences while working at the service station. Many of them I am quite ashamed of, while some have been very helpful in life. I was just not capable of discerning which ones were making a positive impact on me, and which ones were causing me great pain. Without having truth-tellers that I walked with in life, things would continue to spiral.

Throughout high school, my free-spirited life would continue to intensify. The weekends of drinking and partying began to expand into the weekdays. There were times when I would get home just a few hours before it was time to go back to work or school. I never missed a day of work or school due to my partying, but there were days my productivity level was subpar.

My weekends began to be on a routine. When work was over, I would pick up my date for the evening, and we would hang out at the latest party. Other times, it would be spent hanging out with one or two of my guy friends. We would cruise around town, and after having had plenty to drink, we would be looking for a fight to get into. Never did I fear for my life during these times. Fighting was one way I dealt with the anger that was inside me. We did not threaten each other with guns. Only once did I see someone pull a knife out during a fight. It was more about who was the better man in battle.

Little Boozie

Most often, we would just hang out and be stupid around each other. Working at the station brought the added benefit of meeting and befriending many of the police officers in our area. My dad also knew many of them as drinking buddies, and they would invite me to join them at a local beer depot on my way home. The fact that Dad and I were known by these friends as Boozie and Little Boozie should have been a clue to me that my life was way off center. It would take a bigger wake-up call for that to happen.

Oftentimes, one friend who was a police officer working the evening shift would recognize my car while we were driving around late at night. He would turn his lights on to pull us over. As he walked up to greet us, he could tell we had been drinking too much, and would have us get in his squad car and drive us around until we sobered up. When he felt we were okay, he would drive back to my car and follow us home. I am sure he was thinking he was helping my dad, but looking back, he would have helped me by taking measures that were more drastic.

One Saturday night, we would not be so lucky and protected by the police. My friends Eddie and Terry and I, along with some girls, were riding downtown after a high school football game. Terry was an offensive lineman on our school's football team and had had a great game that night, so we were celebrating extra hard. We were also feeling indestructible. As I pulled up to stop at a red light, a car full of guys from the west end pulled up beside us. We began yelling at each other, and when the light turned green, both cars began to pull over to the side of the road so we could settle our disagreements.

During this confrontation, I failed to notice a police car sitting behind us at the traffic light. The officers inside had seen everything, and on came the blue lights. The police officers walked up to my car, realized we were drunk, and made us exit the car. The officers told the girls who were with us to leave and find a way home. The police then invited my two friends and me to go downtown with them and visit the jail. They handcuffed us, put us in the back of the squad car, and drove to the police station.

On the way to the station, Terry kept mouthing off to the police officers. The officers had let the other car of guys go free, maybe because we were in their territory, and Terry did not think that was fair. We made it to the police station and proceeded to the elevator on the way to the booking area. While in the elevator, Terry continued to yell at the officers. One of the officers had enough of Terry's mouth, stopped the elevator mid-floor, and began to take the handcuffs off Terry's wrists. The wrestling match that followed was the second time in my life I felt something bad was going to happen. Eddie and I were constantly scooting around the small elevator trying to avoid being smashed or struck by a stray punch. Eventually, the officer pinned Terry to the ground and put the handcuffs back on. He then helped Terry stand up, pushed the elevator button to continue, and when the door opened, we all walked out of the elevator as if nothing had happened.

The officers sat us in a waiting room near the booking desk. The woman working the desk began to call us up one at a time. When she called my name, I walked to the desk, and she asked, "Are you Frank Head's son?" I responded, "Yes ma'am." She then told the officer he could take the cuffs off me. She had the officer direct me to a chair off to the side. In the meantime, the officers took Terry and Eddie away, as I sat wondering what would happen next.

An hour or so later, the woman at the booking desk told me to come see her. I walked up to her desk, and she said,

"Robert, someone is at the front door to pick you up and take you home. And I don't ever want to see you here again." I simply responded, "Yes ma'am, you won't, thank you." I turned around and walked out of the police station.

To be honest, I do not remember who took me home that night. Not sure if it was the fear or the alcohol. It could not have been Dad though, because the car I had been driving was his, and it was now sitting at the impound lot.

As a family, we never talked about the logistics of that night, other than the trouble I was in and the money I needed to hand over to get the car out of the impound lot. Moreover, I never felt bold enough to bring it up. Here is my guess: The woman at the booking desk somehow knew Dad, perhaps from the service station where he worked. She wanted to help teach me a lesson and yet not be too hard on me. I think she must have called our home, and explained the situation to Dad. Then Dad asked her to put me on a bus, but she told him she would get me home. It intrigues me to this day that Dad was home to receive the call and that I cannot remember who drove me home that night.

It is so interesting when we observe life looking back. I believe God was with me all through that night. He protected me, He put people in my life to help me, and He convicted me in the process. All through my junior and senior years of high school, there would be times when I was far from God and running even further away, but the stories Mrs. Wright had shared with me would convict me and keep me from a very hardened heart.

Another reminder came the day after my police station experience. I had promised myself that I would never be an alcoholic like my dad. That was a wake-up call for me. College would look different for Little Boozie. However, there was still a long, hard road ahead.

Reflection Questions

1. How have you defined love? Where and how did you arrive at this definition?

2. Where does your self-worth come from? Is it based on people pleasing or working hard, or have you just given up altogether? Where does God's promise that you are dearly loved fit in with your self-worth?

3. Do you have truth-tellers helping you on your journey, or those telling you to "have fun while you can"? If you have both, which ones do you typically listen to?

Chapter 6

Moving On

By college, my life began to look quite different. My drinking faded away. I even slowed way down on dating. For the first time, I really enjoyed school, and things felt a little more normal. Even though my mind was getting less fuzzy from the absence of alcohol and marijuana, my addiction to porn was still there. That struggle continued daily.

It seemed that while some of the chaos in my life was gone thanks to my new surroundings, the emptiness inside became more intense, which resulted in a deeper desire to fix or medicate it. I just did not have the tools to deal with the emptiness I felt in a healthy way. Therefore, porn would continue to be the way I dealt with my brokenness. When back at home in my parents' house, I would continue to view and hide porn magazines. In addition, during this time, television was becoming less restrictive, and while there was not porn on our TV, there was plenty to see and imagine that allowed my thoughts to go to very unhealthy places.

As my brain became clearer from the lack of alcohol and marijuana, the fantasies in my head increased and started to interfere with my day-to-day reality. The subjects of these fantasies would come from scenes I had seen on TV, women I saw walking down the street or in a store, or the girl I happened to be sitting next to in class. I never thought of myself as a multitasker, but I was simultaneously focusing on inappropriate thoughts and fantasies in my head while completing some challenging tasks in the real world. Sometimes, it would be difficult to study because the fantasy that was playing out in my head was much more exciting than the words I was trying to understand in my textbook.

The shame I felt because I could not control my fantasy life grew more intense. Not being able to control this secret sin led me to believe I had become a worthless individual. The belief that I was a shameful person became a reality in my life and had devastating results. Of course, that reality did not deter my desire to stop looking at porn. At times, I would use it as an excuse to view porn, believing I was a shameful person and that that was what shameful people do. And there were times when the guilt of what I was doing drove me to try harder, and I would stop for a period. A sense of real freedom and peace would fill me when I was able to abstain from my addiction. But after many relapses, my hope of freedom from this secret sin became fainter. My will power just was not strong enough. As author John Ortberg once said, "Habits eat willpower for breakfast." By now, my habit (addiction) was eating away at my willpower every day.

I survived my first year at a community college in Louisville. I entered community college with a goal of transferring to the University of Louisville's J. B. Speed

School of Engineering and working toward an engineering degree. During that first year, I met a friend named Dale while taking a biology class. After class, Dale and I would often hang out, and one day, he shared with me that he was transferring to the University of Kentucky to work on a degree in forestry. The more he shared about the program, the more it seemed to fit with my love for the outdoors. I would eventually switch degrees. This change to earning an associate degree would get me out of college sooner and cost me a lot less money, since I was responsible for paying for my schooling.

For my second year of college, I packed my bags and traveled to eastern Kentucky where the University of Kentucky had set up its associate degree program in a little town called Quicksand. This little dot on the map is a few miles from Jackson and about 30 miles north of Hazard. It was the most remote area I had ever experienced. There were 18 of us in the program, which included one woman.

We lived in mobile homes built to resemble dorm living. Each one housed six students, with one small bathroom and one room as a study hall, in addition to three sections with 2 bunks each.. The only doors in the mobile home were the entry door and the bathroom door. Privacy in this otherwise remote area came at a premium. It was the first time I had lived with people who were not my family. New personalities, new cultural backgrounds, and new life experiences were challenges for us all. Even with all the newness that came with "dorm life," I truly enjoyed my time at Quicksand. I think being away from the chaos of home and the stress at the service station was a welcome respite. Each semester consisted of 18 credit hours of classes focused solely on forestry. We lived and breathed forestry with each other and our professors.

I began to attend a Christian church in Jackson each week. One of my professors and his family attended the church, so I didn't feel like a complete outsider. Even though I still struggled with my thoughts, I enjoyed being away from the life I had grown up living. I did feel lonely at times, especially since I had not met any dateable girls in the area.

While at Quicksand, my mom tried to fix me up with a friend's daughter who attended Eastern Kentucky University, about an hour away from Quicksand. I contacted the girl a few times on the phone and decided to visit her one weekend at Eastern. She turned out to be probably the wildest girl I ever dated. She was very much immersed in the party life, which I had already left and was not interested in returning to. I realized then that God was changing some parts of me. I never told Mom about the girl she picked for me to date. She would have been horrified.

Spring break during my year at Quicksand became a life-changer. Michael, a good friend from high school, had been telling me about a girl he was good friends with in Louisville, and he wanted to introduce us. At first, I was reluctant to the idea, because I still had a few months left at Quicksand, and job opportunities were beginning to come open. One of the jobs I was interested in was located in Florida. Weyerhaeuser was a lumber company that owned thousands of acres of tree farms, and I would live in a house among the farms and care for the trees. I remember thinking this would be a good place for me to land. Living in a forest like that would help keep me from the temptations of life. This could be my chance to be free from the guilt and shame I had lived with. Becoming like a woodsy monk if you will. How naïve I was to think a place or location could heal me or save me from myself.

The first Friday night during my spring break, I drove to Louisville to stay at my parents' house for the week. I had been home for a short time when the phone rang. Michael wanted to come by and pick me up so he could take me to see the girl he wanted me to meet. An hour later, Michael and I walked into the Buechel Bowling Lanes, where groups of church bowling leagues were playing. As we walked up to Michael's friends, a beautiful girl with long brown hair wearing a denim jumpsuit turned and walked from the bowling lane where she had just bowled. Michael yelled at Joy as she continued to walk toward us, and in that bowling alley, I was introduced to my future wife.

The day after I met Joy, Michael and I stopped by her home so he could introduce me to her parents. I was not ready to meet them, as I was not dressed well and had grown long hair and a full beard. As we walked into Joy's house, Michael walked up to Joy's dad and said, "Edgar, I want you to meet my friend, Bobby Head." Joy's dad turned around to shake my hand, and as he saw his future son-in-law for the first time, he responded, "Dammit to hell boy, I think you need a shave and a haircut." I came to love that man. He was always encouraging to me as I spent more time at their home. I got a shave and a haircut before Michael and I visited Joy at her home the next day.

Joy and I spent a lot of time together that week. She was different from the other girls I had dated. She seemed to enjoy life without all the drinking and partying. She had a very visible spiritual side I could see — not because of something she did, but because of who she was. Her family life was much different from what I had experienced. They ate dinner together every night and welcomed me to join. It was not just eating a meal, but more about community. We would spend an hour or so just talking.

During that week, Joy invited me to attend a retreat that her youth group was having that following weekend at Otter

Creek State Park. I did not have plans, so I agreed to attend. Besides, I really wanted to spend more time with her. The 10 or so of us attending the retreat met at Clifton Baptist Church on Friday evening and traveled via the church bus to Otter Creek. It was a very enjoyable weekend. It quickly became clear to me that Joy was not completely comfortable with me being around just yet. On our way home from the retreat, we sat in the back of the bus and for the first time held hands as we drove home. Joy, being shy and unsure of me, covered our hands with the jacket she had been wearing. Maybe she feared the ridicule that might happen when her friends found out about us.

Joy and I double dated for the first three months. She would later tell me that she was afraid of me because of my reputation, but also had a crush on me since grade school. We talked about many things during our lengthy phone conversations, but I was never able to share with her about my sexual struggles.

While back at school, I traveled home most weekends to spend time with Joy and would often get up early on Monday mornings and drive the two and a half hours to Quicksand in time for my 8 a.m. class. The following summer, my time at Quicksand ended. I moved back home and returned to the service station where I worked before my schooling, and spent most nights at Joy's house.

While dating Joy, I accepted a job with a logging company that was located in Edinburgh, Indiana. My roommate from college, Dale, took a job with the same company, and together we rented an apartment in Edinburgh to begin the arduous career in the logging business. The days were long and hard, and we typically came home exhausted, ate dinner, and then went straight to bed.

Due to a combination of the hard work and missing Joy, my logging career ended after three months. I moved back home and back to the service station. Each time I returned to these places, it was as if I never left. Things never seemed to change. Dad was still struggling, and the service station filled me with stress and anxiety.

The high point of my day was getting off work, going to Joy's home for dinner, and hanging out. It was the most stability I had experienced in my life, and I cherished every minute of it. Together we enjoyed hanging out at her home, watching TV, and talking. However, there were challenges along the way. Joy belonged to a very loyal youth group at her church. It was common for us to be at her home watching TV together when six or eight of her friends from church would pop in and want to hang out with her parents and us. I quickly found out that Joy's house was the landing spot for all her friends. That was very difficult for me at first. At my home, we had an unwritten rule that you did not invite people to your house, much less let them drop in.

I began attending church with Joy at Clifton Baptist Church where she had grown up. It was a small, aging church. The youth group consisted mostly of children from these long-standing members. It was really like a large family. Joy and I had many friends there that were our parents' age or older. They became a combination of parent figures and friends to us. Joy and I sang in the choir with them and hosted fish fries, and I played golf and fished with some of the older men.

There was one problem, though. We only saw what they wanted us to see. These church members seemed to have perfect lives, perfect marriages, and perfect faiths. Maybe they were trying to mentor and show us what a mature life in Christ should look like, but I never heard about any struggles, marital issues they were having, or any challenges with their faith. This was very difficult for me as a 20-something young man who had a strong sexual addiction. I remember praying to God one time, saying to Him, "If this is who and what I am supposed to be like as a Christian, you might as well kill me now and get it over with." Many times, I felt hopeless, knowing that I could never become what I felt God wanted me to be. Oh, I so often wished I could talk to one of the men about my struggles. They wouldn't understand. They wouldn't like me. I was the only one struggling this way. These are just a few of the lies that Satan had me believing.

I never joined Clifton Baptist Church, even though I went there for years, drove the church bus, sang in the choir, served communion, and got married there. The pastor, Brother Bob, whom I loved, asked me one day if I wanted to join the church. I responded with, "I guess so.' He then asked, "Have you been baptized?" I responded, "I was christened as a baby in the Catholic Church and then baptized at Crescent Hill Christian Church when I accepted Christ as my Savior." He then said to me, "Then we would need to baptize you again since you weren't baptized in a like-faith church." I responded, "I thought Baptism was about accepting Christ as my Savior, not about joining a certain denomination." The conversation quickly ended. I believe he agreed with me, but was also committed to following the Church's rules and regulations.

Joy and I dated for four years. During that time, I changed careers. I began working at a place called Lyndon Mill, utilizing some of what I had learned in the forestry program at the University of Kentucky. I spent most of my time there building custom furniture. John, who owned Lyndon Mill, found me through a decorator friend of my mother's, and he invited me to come for a week and try it out. I took my one-week vacation from the service station and went to work in the lumber mill. At the end of the week, John offered me a job, and I accepted.

Joy and I both liked the new job because for the first time in my working life, I only worked five days a week for a total of 40 hours. It was good to get away from the chaos of the service station, even though I was still working around men living very worldly lives. My career path led me to be around very worldly people, while my personal life would lead me to godly people who seemed beyond my reach. It would be years before I was introduced to people who acknowledged their brokenness to a broken person like myself.

During our four years of dating, Joy and I became very comfortable with each other. So much so that her Aunt Mattie, who was very outspoken, came to us one day and let us know of her frustration with our dating situation. She asked Joy and me, "When are you two going to get married?" Joy and I stumbled to give her an answer, which caused Mattie to respond, "You two either need to shit or get off the pot." That was the push we needed. Soon after our encouragement from Aunt Mattie, I proposed to Joy, in her bathroom, while she was washing her hair. She responded with a "yes," and the wedding plans began.

Reflection Questions

1. Have you been able to stop some poor behaviors in your life, only to understand there was another one left that was more powerful than you ever knew? What feelings did that realization give you?

2. How many times have you thought a change of scenery or a new relationship would help you overcome an addiction or challenge you were facing? What were the results of doing so?

3. Have you had times in your life where your addiction seems to have gone away, only to resurface even stronger down the road? Can you describe these times?

Chapter 7

Shattered Dreams

On May 23, 1981, Joy and I were married at Clifton Baptist Church in Louisville, Kentucky. It was a traditional wedding with cake and ice cream in the basement of the church. Joy was a beautiful bride, and I wore basketball socks under my tuxedo. All of Joy's cousins from Atlanta came, and we all had a great time. Joy's dad Edgar had a keg of beer delivered to their home, and after the reception at the church, the family congregated at Joy's home to continue the party. After a while, Joy and I left and drove to Lexington, Kentucky for our two-day honeymoon. Some friends of ours from the Baptist Seminary joined us one day, and we all went to the Kentucky Horse Park.

It was a little awkward for me that weekend. I had never been with a girl less experienced than me. The problem was that for me, sex was still sex. I had not learned that sex is an intimacy that grows from a loving relationship between a husband and wife. That it is an act that flows from loving each other, rather than an act meant to get some kind of love or fulfillment. This would become a challenge for us for years.

You learn a lot about each other once you are married. At the end of our first week together, we had our first fight. Sunday morning, we were getting ready to leave our home for church. I think in the dating stage, we often overlook the things that will later irritate us once we are married. One of the irritating things about Joy I overlooked during our dating was timeliness. To me, being on time is arriving to my destination five minutes early. For Joy, being on time is showing up during the event. The approval of others has always been so important to me, and being early is one way I have tried to win others' approval. Joy grew up with a much slower pace of life than I did, and time was not as crucial to her. She has told me if she dies first, I am to begin the funeral 15 minutes late. She wants to stay consistent with how she lives her life.

After much impatient waiting for Joy on my part, I backed the car out of the driveway, and we headed to church. As I turned from our street, Joy excitedly said, "We have to turn around and go back!"

I responded, "Why? We are already going to be late for church."

Joy fired back, "I forgot my wedding ring."

I loudly snapped back, "We are going to the church we just got married in. They all know we are married because they were at the wedding."

To which Joy meekly responded, "I don't care, I want to wear my new wedding ring to church."

Joy was beginning to see a part of me she did not know existed: my anger. I slammed the brakes on our 1979 Mercury Marquis and screeched to a full stop. I then threw the car in reverse and floored the gas pedal, causing the rear tires to screech again. As smoke filled the air, I began backing up to our street at breakneck speed, when a car decided to pull out of a side street in front of us. I guess they had never seen a car going backwards extremely fast, and it confused them. To keep from hitting them head on (or in this case rear on), I swerved to miss them and proceeded to side swipe a parked car.

By the time the car came to a full stop, we were both crying. For me, it was out of the shame I felt for letting my anger get the best of me again. For Joy, it was out of fear for her life and fear of whom she just married. We never made it to church that day, but we saw something in each other that would be challenging for much of our marriage.

In our second year of marriage, we had an opportunity to live in Oklahoma City for three and a half months. The FAA selected me to attend their air traffic control academy in Oklahoma City in hopes of becoming an air traffic controller. We both quit our jobs in Louisville, packed our bags, and for the first time, we were all alone as a couple. No family, friends, or coworkers. We lived in an apartment complex that housed other air traffic students. Those three and half months were the purest I had experienced in my life. In other words, instead of filling my mind with lustful thoughts, I was filling it with airplanes and equations. I don't think it was anything I intentionally did. I believe it was the stress of the academy and the focus that was required to get through the program. I would not realize that I had the ability to make a choice about my thoughts until years later.

After successfully completing the FAA Academy, we were able to return to Louisville, and I began my career as an air traffic controller at Bowman Field Airport. Joy picked up a job as a dental assistant, and life returned to the way it was before we left. But it didn't take long for me to become bored and complacent with life as I settled into my career. One day while driving home from the tower, the realization that I was becoming depressed and frustrated with my life became clear. I had spent my life fixing or building things with my hands. At the end of a day, I could physically see something I had accomplished. With air traffic, that was completely different. Yes, I helped many airplanes land safely and helped to get them where they wanted to go, but I still wanted something more tangible.

I began to build furniture again, this time in my garage. At first, it was for our own use, but people began to ask me to build furniture for them and often wanted to purchase things I had built. Once, I sold our kitchen cabinets hanging from the kitchen walls to a neighbor. Their kitchen had a similar layout to ours, so one afternoon, I unscrewed the cabinets from our kitchen, carried them next door, and screwed them to their kitchen walls. Of course, I made new and better cabinets for our kitchen, and Joy was always patient with my dealings.

However, one time, she was not so pleased with me. I was meeting with a client about building an entertainment center for their home. As we walked through our house (which had become our showroom), they noticed the dining room suite I had made. They inquired about purchasing the suite, and after agreeing on a price, we loaded the furniture into my truck and delivered it on the spot. All while Joy was out shopping with a friend.

When Joy returned home from her shopping trip and noticed our empty dining room, she was not happy with me at all. She marched out to the shop where I had begun to work again and demanded, "What happened to our dining room furniture?"

"I sold it," I responded.

Joy then asked, "So where are we going to eat?"

I simply responded, "I will build an even better dining room suite." Which I did a few years later.

In the meantime, we ate in our tiny kitchen. Eventually, designers and decorators found out about me and began to order custom furniture. Wood Designs became a full-fledged business.
The woodworking did fulfill my need to work with my hands and to be creative, but it also brought a lot of negative impacts with it. I did not completely understand these negative effects for years.
Being a people pleaser and desiring to be accepted, my woodworking allowed me the opportunity to earn that acceptance. At least, I thought so at some level. The problem was that feeling of acceptance was fleeting. Every job brought a new opportunity to earn acceptance, because the previous feeling had left the station. It was exhausting. It brought great anxiety, always worrying whether a client would like what I built for them. The reality, which I learned years later, was that the worry was based on if they would accept me.

One day, while I was sitting with Chris, my counselor, sharing this newly discovered fact, he asked, "So in 20 years of your woodworking business, how many times have clients rejected your work?" My sad response was, "Never, but tomorrow someone might, and that would be devastating." I put so much of my worth in the hands of other people and my ability to earn it from them. That began many years ago when, as a child, I struggled with my worth and whether God and others loved me. Therefore, I needed to learn a way to make them love me.

The woodworking business also allowed me to continue my workaholic attitude. I would often explain it away as a need to provide for my family. After all, there was a house and car to pay for, a young daughter to take care of, and college to save for. On the outside, it almost made sense to have two careers. However, in reality, either career would have provided all we needed. No, we would not be wealthy by western world standards, but we would have had plenty, whichever career I chose. In addition, having one career would have allowed me to be home more and experience family life. That idea also brought me great fear. What if I did stay home, and the love was not there? This thought was not new to me, as I had grown up with it and wanted to avoid it at all costs.

My woodworking business continued to thrive and grow. As it did so, I brought my brother in as a partner and hired employees from time to time, eventually adding my dad to the workforce. My friend Allen, who I had known since grade school, took care of all our staining and finishing work. That allowed us to continue building the next project while Allen was finishing the previous one. We had gotten so busy at times, I would advise future clients that we could not begin their project for a year. Most of them, surprisingly, waited.

As the business grew, I worked in the wood shop less and less. As I spent most of my time with clients, focusing on designing and paperwork, I once went two years without ever turning on a saw and cutting a piece of wood. It became more and more frustrating, and I became more and more angry. In the end, no one could stand to work with me except Dad, and I eventually went to a two-man shop.

Owning my business also gave me a lot of freedom, with no accountability. If I was not home, Joy thought I was either at the tower or involved in the woodworking business. For most of my career, this was true, but eventually, it led to major trouble for me.

On June 6, 1985, Joy and I had our only child, Jenny. Joy and Jenny came home from the hospital on my birthday. It was and will always be the greatest birthday present I ever received. Joy and I were so excited over our baby girl. I began to experience love in a new way. Here was a baby girl who was dependent on her mom and dad for everything for her survival. Joy had had a very easy pregnancy, and we were naively expecting this ease to continue.

Jenny will always be my little girl whom I love dearly and unconditionally. She faced some challenges as a baby. It took a lot of crying and sleepless nights before the doctors discovered she had milk allergies, and we learned what kind of milk to feed her. It was especially hard on Joy when the doctor told her Jenny was rejecting her milk also. As we found milk that Jenny could tolerate, a new kind of crying developed. Jenny began having a series of ear infections. The doctors eventually decided to put tubes in her ears. Oh, and did I say she cried all the time?

Moreover, as if those challenges were not enough, the doctors discovered Jenny was born with a hip click that required double diapering (which clearly was not comfortable and caused more irritation), and feet that toed in. Not the pigeon-toed kind — her actual feet were bowed. This required her to have casts on both feet up to her knee. The casts had to be replaced each week as her feet began to straighten. Before they could be replaced, I would soak both legs in vinegar water and unravel the plaster/cloth casts. Oftentimes pulling as hard as I could while supporting her legs to get them unraveled. I was in constant fear that I would pull her leg out of its socket, or worse.

Several months later, the doctor released us, as Jenny's feet were finally straight. I know many parents have gone through a lot worse with their young children, but for us, it was a challenge and strain on our marriage. For me, it was how I handled it and dealt with the stress that had the most impact on our marriage.

Jenny's first year was a blur. Joy and I both lived in a state of exhaustion from lack of sleep. Joy would stay up with Jenny during the week so I could be alert when I went to work at the control tower. On the weekends, I would take over so Joy could get some rest. Even when we were getting rest, the crying of a hurting baby often interrupted it. Of course, there was not any quality time for Joy and me; even if we had the time, we would not have had the energy to enjoy it. For two people who spent their young marriage loving each other at arm's length due to our own brokenness, this season only made the arms longer.

Please do not misunderstand; I have never blamed Jenny's early challenges on what followed in our marriage. Our brokenness happened long before she came along. I in particular was a very broken human being who did not realize how severely he was broken. As the years went by, Joy and I became more and more distant. Our conversation remained at a surface level, not that it had ever been very deep. We were both afraid to go deeper and did not really know how. We were becoming two people who lived separate lives in the same home with a young daughter. I went to work, and Joy took care of Jenny and the house. My anger became more pronounced by my raised voice, stern ways, and verbal abuse that Joy endured. In a more passive way, my abuse was evident by my absence at home. This, ironically, was the same absence that I experienced from my dad, as a little boy.

Amazingly, during this time, I still had the energy to run to porn. If anything, my time with it increased, even if it was only fantasizing. Then, when computers and the internet came along, my addiction worsened at warp speed. I also learned to use a program on the computer to draw the furniture we were building in the business and began maintaining our company's transactions on the computer. While this was a huge help to our business and saved me a lot of time, I would find that the time saved would become time wasted using the same tool in a different way. This was long before internet filters and screen accountability software were developed, so I had free reign at the computer. It was devastating, time-wasting, and relationship suicide. In some ways, I wonder if today's social media, while maybe not pornographic, may have a similar result for some individuals and their marriages.

There is an old saying that goes like this: "Sin will take you farther than you want to go, keep you longer than you want to stay, and cost you more than you want to pay." This was a good description for the sexual sin in my life. In my desire to be loved, I began to write my own definition of what love was, and pornography played a huge role in that definition. Since pornographic images have no real relationship attachment to them, it led me on a constant search to find the next best fix. It was never ending.

There is another old saying that goes something like this: "Sin has an appetite about it. It takes more and more to be satisfied." I became more and more obsessed with pornography. I spent more time searching for it and fantasizing about it. I found myself going through my daily routines even while the fantasies continued to play out in my mind. Joy and I continued to grow apart as I was growing weaker.

We had moved farther away from the church where we had been married. After Jenny was born, we began attending a Baptist church that was closer to our home. Joy and I both loved the pastor and the people in the church. We joined and quickly became part of the community. At some point, the church wanted to ordain me as a deacon. To this day, I am not sure why I accepted; maybe I thought becoming a deacon would bring me closer to God, and He might love me. Yes, I had times of sexual purity when I was not looking at porn, but the pull was always there. After becoming a deacon and attending deacon meetings, I became even more disheartened. These were supposed to be the Godliest men in the church, and to witness the bickering and manipulating that went on did nothing to heal my struggle with God. Oh, and by the way, I was one of them.

Years went by, and we began to attend another church. Things had not changed much at home or in my heart. Eventually, a female coworker began to show interest in me, and that seemed to bring life to my broken state. I knew it was wrong from the beginning, but I desperately wanted to feel loved. Eventually, I would give in to an adulterous relationship. The guilt and shame grew heavier every day. There were times I would try to stop but eventually give in to her persistence. Many times, I would audibly yell at God while driving in my truck going to meet her. "If you really love me, make me turn around and go home. I can't do this by myself." His response never seemed to come.

Life began getting darker and more hopeless for me. The reality that I could not control things in my life began to set in. I asked myself, "If I cannot control them, then who can?" No answer came. More and more, I began to give up on God. Rising from bed each morning became very difficult. I felt hopeless, knowing that it was not *if* I was going to fall into sin, but *when* and *how far*. I knew I was hurting everyone around me, including God and myself, and I could not do anything about it. Satan was winning.

One morning, I woke up and decided it was time to fix this once and for all. I thought to myself, "Since my life is in total shambles, and no one seems to care about me, why should I keep this up any longer? I will just end my life, and it will be better for everyone." Therefore, I began to plan how I would commit suicide. I was exhausted from living a double life and keeping up with all the lies that I had told to maintain my secret life. I was hopeless.

I have always loved automobile racing and driving fast, and that seemed to be the most natural way for me to carry out my plan. I worked late at the control tower a few nights a week, and traffic was always light or nonexistent at the time I came home. One night coming home, I picked out a large tree on the edge of Taylorsville Road where I would be able to pick up enough speed and seemingly lose control and crash into the tree. This way would not surprise many people, as they knew I was an aggressive driver. Night after night, the urge grew stronger to carry out my plan and end this miserable life and pain.

Then, God stepped in.

Reflection Questions

1. Name some times in your life when you brought fear to someone or yourself from living in your brokenness.

2. Have you ever ran or hidden from life as a way of escaping the pain you were living in? Are you doing that now?

3. Is leading a double life causing you to feel hopeless? If so, has God been convicting you of your double life? How so?

Chapter 8

The Confrontation

Joy discovered my affair. After completing some detective work by checking my cell phone records, she knew something was not right. But could she get me to confess? I had become an expert liar and manipulator. I had also grown extremely weary from living in secret sin.

When she confronted me about having an affair while on a walk, I took a long time to respond. Part of me was trying to see if I could manipulate my way out of the mess I had created, and the other part of me wanted to be free of the secrets and the sin. When we returned home from our walk, I confessed to Joy that she was correct, and I was having an affair. Of course, it hurt her deeply. I had betrayed our wedding vows, broken her trust, and completely shattered her world. Even as I admitted to the affair, I was still trying to protect my image and asked Joy who all she was going to tell. She was not sure what her next step would be, but the following day, she called church and got an appointment for us with Rich, who would be our crisis counselor. After a few meetings with the counselor and me ending the affair, Joy said she wanted to work on our marriage.

She did not trust me anymore and was not ready to forgive me, but was willing to give our marriage a second try. As we left the first meeting with the counselor, I felt a huge weight lifted off of my shoulders. For the first time, a sense of hope returned. I remember leaving the session thinking, "I want to be the best husband and Christ follower ever." I was going to work very hard at accomplishing them both. That is exactly what I did; I began working hard. But looking back, I realize we were only putting a Band-Aid on a very serious wound.

The days seemed to get better for Joy and me. We were working hard to connect with each other, even though neither of us knew what that could really look like. We were walking into new territory that we hadn't experienced before, and we didn't know what to expect. As a result, we continued to talk at a surface level and did not have much quality conversation. I take responsibility for that because I did not try to learn and research something that I knew nothing about. I am typically a very good researcher. Even to a fault at times, with my obsessing over what topic I happen to be researching. I guess that is partly why I was so good at finding porn. In essence, we were still living our separate lives. Joy was focused on being a great mom to Jen (which she was), and involved deeply in school activities. I was still hiding in my work through the control tower and woodworking business.

Even though I continued to struggle with pornography during this time, I was not engaged in extramarital activity. However, two years into our "recovery," I was about to fall into the same trap. Joy and I had continued to grow distant,

The Confrontation

and the woman I had the affair with called me again. I so wanted to be loved and did not know how to respond to that need in a healthy way.

On December 27, 2001, Joy and I were home, resting after a few busy days around Christmas time. Joy had a headache and went into our bedroom to take a nap. I didn't realize this at the time, but my two years of white knuckling it, trying to do things on my own, was about to come to a head. I walked into our kitchen where a telephone was hanging on a wall by the refrigerator. I picked up the phone and dialed the woman's number, and we began to talk. It was not a long conversation, but at one point, we began discussing if we could meet. I had not even realized Joy had picked up the telephone extension in the bedroom and was listening to what was being said. Then, I heard her voice in the phone yelling that we could meet wherever we wanted, which was followed by a loud click as she slammed the phone. I quickly grasped what had just happened and immediately hung up the phone and began wailing. I ran into the bedroom, falling to my knees and profusely apologizing to Joy. She was furious with me.

She got up from the bed and began walking through the hall that led to the living room and front door. I followed closely, continuing to plead with her. As we approached the foyer, she turned to me with tears running down her cheeks and began to express just how much I had hurt her and how angry she was with me. She continued by saying she was not sure she could do this anymore, and then this meekest of all women squarely punched me in the gut. The fact that my loving, mild-mannered wife punched me, as a professional boxer would, let me know it was time to shut up. Joy verbalized a few more comments about the situation and said she wanted some space. She went downstairs to the family room, and I returned to our bedroom.

Upon entering the bedroom, in my weariness, I literally fell flat on the carpeted floor. Tears still flowing, I began to cry out to God. Not in anger like I had in the past, but in a desperate, hopeless way. I expressed to God how tired and lonely I had felt all my life. How exhausted I was from years of trying to stop a behavior I knew was sinful and hurting everyone around me, including Him and myself. I told God that I was giving up on trying to fix this addiction. I was at the end, and I had nowhere else to go.

If life was going to change, it would be God's doing, not mine. I knew my part of this moving forward was to surrender to Him so that He could work in me. If you had asked me throughout my life if I had surrendered my will to Christ, my response would have been an emphatic "yes." I would have also been lying to you. Maybe not on purpose, but because I did not know what true surrender looked like. Conditional surrender — maybe. Partial surrender — probably. Temporary surrender — most definitely.

I know I have spoken words like these in my heart:

"God, I'm going to stop this for a month, and surely the temptation will go away then."

"God, if you do this, then I will stop that."

And "God, I will do this so you can help me."

For me I had to learn when surrendering to God the only time the word "I" would be used was to say, "I surrender all". Every other time when that word entered a sentance, it told

The Confrontation

me that I had taken the steering wheel back and was doing life on my own. Yes, "I" would be involved when God led me down a path that offered me a choice to follow or not. Yes, "I" would be involved when God put people in my life to walk with in my addiction and I had the freedom to follow their guidance or not. Yes, "I" is involved every day when God confronts me in broken areas of my heart that He wants to mend and gives me the choice to open up to Him or stay protected from the fears that go with it. And yes, "I" is involved every new day when God invites me to follow Him and walk in his strength, not mine. All of these "I's" are the beginning of a statement that says, "I surrender all."

I also needed to remember that surrender is not a one-time expression but a daily release to the God who loves us in ways that our human mind cannot comprehend. What I have learned is that these "I's" are responses to God's leading and prodding in His desire to make me holy, and do not come out of fear that His hammer is going to drop on me to condemn me. They are also not my feeble attempts at surviving or becoming more spiritual and loved by God. He already loves me as much as He can. There is nothing I can or cannot do to make Him love me more. I was finally ready to let God have control of my life.

I was sharing this night of surrender with my friend Joe some years later and explaining how it began to change my heart and life. He responded to my explanation by saying, "And all you did was give up?" I simply said, "Yes." I went on to explain to him that it was also the most difficult thing I had ever done and that I get to repeat it every day. Giving up my pride was and is very difficult. Along with my pride, I was giving up the tools I used to navigate through life to help deal with the false beliefs that had been guiding me. They were also the very things that were about to lead me to an early death. God wanted to begin stripping all this cancer away, and as I surrendered, the painful surgery began.

As I continued to lie on the bedroom floor that night, a peace began to fill my soul. In the most chaotic and uncertain time in my life, this peace began to consume me as I have never witnessed. I confessed to God my deepest brokenness and sinfulness. I confessed the selfish life I had lived. Then I confessed that my first 42 years had been all about Bob, and from this moment on, I wanted to surrender to His will and what He wants to do in my life.

I also confessed to God that I was not sure I could trust Him, but had nowhere else to turn. If it did not work out, I would always go back to plan A, because the tree on Taylorsville Road was still standing. Again, I was sharing this with my friend Joe one day and said that I knew it was not good theology to test God in this way. Joe responded by saying, "Bob, God wasn't worried about your theology. He was concerned about your heart."

I do not know how long I lay on that bedroom floor, but I do know during that time I finally met and experienced God. Up to that point in my life, I had only read and heard about Him. I had knowledge of who He was and what He is about, but it never seemed to apply to me. I heard many great sermons and read my Bible almost daily but had never connected with Him. I always saw Him as this ruler sitting on His throne in Heaven waiting to convict me of the latest crime I had committed. That never happened, but I still desperately feared it. I was always on trial.

I do not know how, and did not realize at the time that it would take the rest of my life, but my life began to change that night on the bedroom floor. I eventually got up; I think God grabbed me by my britches and lifted me up, brushed

The Confrontation

me off, and said, "Let's go live the life I have planned for you. And we will do it together."

I walked out of my bedroom, knowing what lay ahead was completely out of my control. Would I stay married? Would I lose my job? What would life with my daughter look like if all this happened? The unknowns were many; yet there was a calm and peace that filled me that I did not know was possible.

The next day, we were back at our counselor Rich's office. As Joy and I explained the recent events, Rich asked if there was anything else I needed to confess. After a few minutes, I came clean. I responded with, "Yes, I have also struggled with porn since I was 12 years old." To which Rich replied, "You need to start attending ARC (Addicts Redeemed in Christ)." I asked Rich what ARC was. He responded, "It is a Christian 12-step program for sex addicts that meets on Saturday mornings." I explained to Rich that I worked on Saturday mornings, so I could not attend the meetings. He simply responded, "Then you need to quit your job. And Joy, you should throw his clothes out on the front lawn and kick him out until he gets help." He then gave us the number of Chris Wood, one of the counselors at church who specialized in addictions. Just like that, the meeting was over.

It was a long three-mile ride home that day. I was afraid to say anything, and Joy was severely hurt, saddened, and angry over what she had just heard. When we returned home, Joy asked me if I was going to call Chris. I affirmed to her that I was, and we then went separate directions in the house. I did call Chris and was able to set up an appointment in two days. Some hours later, Joy and I met in the living room and began to talk. Joy asked me if I wanted to be married to her still, and I assured her I did. She then said if I would get help and if we would work on improving our marriage, she would stay, too. She also said that she did not know if she could ever trust me again. I let her know that I had made an appointment with Chris in two days, and if she would give me a chance, I would do whatever she needed of me to help earn her trust, even if it took the rest of my life. And I truly meant that. I was so relieved that there was still hope for us.

We discussed boundaries and tasks that Joy thought would help her moving forward. I gladly agreed to every one of them. They consisted of things like me not having any contact with the other woman, having a filter installed on the computer, and moving the computer to an upstairs room that allowed Joy to see the monitor as she walked by the hallway. With the woodworking business requiring me to travel around town giving estimates, installing cabinetry, and picking up materials, Joy was not comfortable not knowing where and what I was doing. This was during the early stages of cell phones, and I had recently bought one to use at the shop. To help Joy be at ease with my time away, we agreed that I would call her and let her know where my next destination was, how long it would take me to get there, and the phone number of the location I was going to. Upon leaving each location, I would repeat the process. I believe agreeing to these and a few more requests from Joy helped her to know how serious I was about recovery and our marriage. It also gave her some peace along our journey of healing.

Two days later, I was in Chris's office.

Reflection Questions

1. Looking back on your life, do you think God has put people or circumstances before you to confront some beliefs or doubts you may have toward Him? How have you responded to His confrontation?

2. Have you reached a rock bottom moment in your life? Do you see one coming? Describe it.

3. What boundaries have you included in your day to help you live more like Christ? Are there additional boundaries you need to implement?

Chapter 9

Sitting in the Hot Seat

I did not know what to expect sitting across from Chris as we began my first counseling session. Would Joy and Chris tell me how terrible of a person I was? I already knew that. Would Chris tell Joy she should divorce me and move on with her life? I was afraid of that. Would Chris tell us our situation was hopeless and I was a worthless human being? That is what I had believed.

Well, none of that happened. Joy and I both cried a lot. Joy shared her hurt and anger toward me, and I apologized again. Chris sat patiently and listened as we poured out our story, explaining how we got there. After we exhausted ourselves, Chris responded by saying he would like to work with us in helping us heal and redeem our marriage. Chris said that if we would invite God into the process, he knew that healing and redemption would happen. His plan was to meet again as a couple and then meet for a time with me by myself. I was obviously the bigger challenge, and I think Chris knew that if I was not allowing the process to do what it could, there was no hope for our marriage. After meeting with me for an unspecified time, he would then meet with Joy and eventually finish up with both of us together. We had a plan.

I mentioned to Chris what Rich had said about ARC and me quitting my job so I could attend the meetings. Chris assured me that was not necessary, and he would direct me to a Sex Addicts Anonymous (SAA) group. These were also 12-step programs modeled after AA. He explained they were happening all around the city at different days and times of the week.

With that, our first counseling session was over. I think we both left Chris's office with some fear and uncertainty, but also a glimmer of hope. We both knew there was a lot of work ahead of us. We were not sure what that would look like and how successful it would be, but we both agreed we wanted to try to make it work. We also agreed with Chris that the three of us alone were not capable of turning this damaged ship around. It was going to take someone more powerful than us. Joy and I both agreed we needed to invite God into our chaos and story if things were going to be different. Not just pay lip service to Him as we both admitted to doing, but to surrender our marriage and ourselves to Him.

Early in the process, I began to experience a monumental truth: My motivation for how I lived my life to this point was actually a lie, and God used my wife to confront me with it. Up to this point in my life, I believed I was unworthy of being loved, and the only chance for me to experience love was to earn it or create in my mind what love should look like. When that did not work, I would numb myself from that reality by drinking or using marijuana. I spent most of my life trying to please people, hoping that I could earn their love. I worked very hard in both of my careers to be accepted and receive the pat on the back I so desperately desired. I withheld my feelings often, thinking if I told someone what I really thought or felt, it would blow any chance of their loving me. When none of this seemed to work, I would run to my addiction.

Yet, at a point in my life when I least deserved to be loved, when I clearly had not earned my wife's love — in fact, I had given her a Biblical reason to divorce me — she chose to love me in my brokenness. She chose to love me unconditionally. Yes, it was terribly difficult for her to love me amidst her hurt and anger. She has told me since that this only happened through the power of God. There were times she could only love me as a brother in Christ, not knowing where my life was heading. She felt she was in a battle for my soul. I would agree with her. Was it perfect love? Of course not. However, her actions helped me to begin to think and believe differently about myself.

To be honest, I was confused by her love. In my mind, it was not supposed to work like that. I did not deserve to be loved. Rich had been right; she should have kicked me out. But she did not. Instead, she chose to love me the best that her human capacity could muster, and trusted God to help her with the rest. I began to question my false belief about love. If my wife in her brokenness as a human can love me unconditionally to the level that she does, then God in His greatness must and does love me deeply and unconditionally! So maybe all the stories I had read in the Bible and heard preached from the pulpit about God's love for all His children were true. True even for me!

Chris would help me understand that I was confronting a false belief system I had created for myself about the truth of

God. This insight began a journey in a different direction for me in my deepest parts. A journey toward living in the truth of God. As a result, I stopped reading the Bible as a way to earn my slot in Heaven and began to allow the Bible to read me and change me into the man God created me to be. Instead of leaving church feeling condemned from the sermon I just heard, I left hearing God letting me know of new areas in which He wanted me to grow so that I could live life to the fullest. This occurred because my wife allowed God to use her in her most challenging time to speak love to one of His little boys who had lost all hope. To speak unconditional love.

I began each day (and still do) meeting and communing with God. During our time in the mornings, I surrender to Him my desires, my addiction, and my will. I pray for my family and others. I thank Him for what He has done for me and what He is going to do. Then I listen. I have been amazed at how talkative God is — not in a demanding, judging way, but in a loving and caring way. While I begin my day this way, it does not stop there. More and more, I want to communicate with God throughout the day. He truly has become my most intimate traveling companion. Do not get me wrong here — I do not always do it well, and it is a constant battle with my pride wanting to take over my life.

Chris also talked to me about communication in marriage. In 20 years of marriage, Joy and I had not gone beyond surface conversation. We did not have any experience going deeper, and my communication style did not help. As a result, we began to address our different communication styles.

I had grown up in a home where a lot of yelling took place and confrontation was a daily event. If you wanted to be heard, you had to be loud and in someone's face. And you never backed down. You kept digging in until you got the result you were after. I called it passion instead of lunacy. Joy, on the other hand, grew up in a very calm atmosphere where voices were not raised and things were discussed in a laid-back manner. You can probably imagine how our first 20 years of communication in our marriage went.

Allow me to paint a picture for you to clarify what I am describing. As Joy and I would discuss an issue, I would become what I called "passionate." My voice would rise, my intensity would heighten, and I would walk closer and closer to Joy until we were nose to nose. In the meantime, Joy was shutting down internally. She became fearful. Eventually, she would turn and walk away. That would frustrate me because I wanted resolution, and of course I always thought I was right. Early in our marriage, I would follow her around the house with my full intensity in trail. I saw her retreating as a sign of weakness. And after years of failing to arrive at a decision during these times, I quit chasing. Our conflict always left us frustrated, angry, and distanced. Without realizing it, this would also be a trigger for me to act out.

During a marriage class we were attending some years later, the instructor talked about our communication styles. To be honest, I thought they had been recording our home. They related it to a bulldozer and a flower garden. Of course, I was the bulldozer during conflict, and would doze over Joy, the flower garden, and smash all of her flowers. After which I would go on my merry way, while Joy's garden was destroyed. It might sound a little silly, but it so resonated with us.

From this visual, we came up with a silly idea. As we were thinking about bulldozers one night, (I had driven some in my forestry days), I was reminded of the beeping sound they make when backing up. Many vehicles do that today.

This led us to an idea to help deal with our communication and conflict dilemma. Wanting to communicate in a healthier way, we agreed that when I became loud and passionate during conflict, Joy would simply say, "beep, beep."

This simple technique helped us in many ways. It would immediately diffuse and lighten the situation. We would often break out in laughter at the sound of Joy's meek "beep, beep." Often I would ask Joy, "Was I really getting loud?" It had been so normal for me to communicate this way, I was not aware it was happening. It also helped Joy to remain in the conflict since the fear did not need to be there anymore. Instead of shutting down and running, she came to realize she did have a voice, even if it did start with "beep, beep."

I am proud to say that I am rarely beeped at anymore, and we continue to grow in how we walk through conflict. I learned you can teach an old dog new tricks. It just takes some time and a desire to learn.

Chris encouraged us to begin a daily couple's devotion to help learn how to communicate at a deeper level. We found a couple's devotional book titled, *Moments Together for Couples* by Dennis and Barbara Rainey and set a time each night to begin. Even that was a challenge at first, as the book walked through a year's worth of devotions beginning on January 1. Joy, being the legalist in our family, became anxious from the start. Where would we start since it was March already? What if we missed a day? As we talked through these and other questions, we came to the agreement that the intent of the book and the devotions was to help us learn to communicate deeply, not to grade us on our disciplinary skills and rule following.

Night after night, we would go to our bedroom and read the verse for the day, followed by a few paragraphs that talked about the verse we had just read. The book then offered two or three questions pertaining to the subject for us to respond to. What made this so attractive to us was that the questions were not coming from either of us. This allowed us both to let down our defenses and not worry about what agenda may be taking place.

It was during these times that Joy and I began to learn so much about each other and ourselves. It only took 20 years of marriage! Did I mention I am a slow learner? I was amazed at the amount of intimate knowledge we learned about each other during our devotions. Things like fears we lived with, beliefs we lived by, and what we had believed about God. To be honest, it made our first 20 years of marriage make more sense.

I cannot explain to you how invaluable that devotion book was and the time we spent each night together. It changed our level of communication. The devotions ended with a prayer, which also helped us to begin to pray for each other aloud. We continue to utilize what we learned from our devotions to grow our marriage today.

I sat in Chris's office week after week, learning more about God and myself. In his soft-spoken voice and mild manner, Chris would help me begin to tear down walls of my heart, brick by brick. Over time, he helped me explore who I am and begin to see at the deepest level the Bob that God created. The Bob that He loved so desperately. That Bob was very different from the one I had created. People began to notice a difference in the way I walked through life. Especially Joy. The angry, highly intense, impatient, uncaring person I had been began to fade away. At first, the difference angered Joy. And for a while, she became angry with God. After all, she had been the faithful one following God's commands. Why did she have to live through all this and have anger, fear, distrust, and uncertainty, while her husband, who had caused all of this chaos, was walking around with a newly found sense of peace, contentment, and calm? She felt God had forgotten her and left her behind. Sure, this is what she had always wanted for me, but she still had to deal with her pain and ask God for help. And she did.

As my counseling progressed, Chris, in the spring of 2002, encouraged me to attend a retreat called Faces of Christ. Our church had been hosting the retreat for a few years, and Chris thought it would be a good next step for my journey. By that time in our relationship, I would have parachuted out of an airplane if Chris thought it would help. I trusted his wisdom and insights very much.

The four-day retreat blew me away. It affirmed much of what Chris and I had been working on and helped me to see God in ways I had not experienced before. Seeing the different Faces of Christ greatly enlarged my belief of who God was. The little box I had kept Him in completely exploded. God was no longer going to allow me to think so little of Him. At one point during the retreat, one of the men walked to the front of the room and began to share his story of sexual addiction with the group. I remember thinking, "Can you really talk about this in public?" It was going against one of my life rules, which was, "Do not let people know your stuff." After all, at this point, only three people knew my stuff — my wife, who found out on her own, our crisis counselor Rich, who wanted Joy to kick me out of the house, and my counselor Chris, who I was spilling my guts to for $80 an hour. How freeing that moment was. By now, I was having freeing moments like this throughout my life. As a result, I felt more alive than ever before.

The retreat also helped me to begin to meet God in a more intimate way. One of the men talked about Christ the forgiver, and another man talked about Christ the healer. To this point in my life, I had only read about these characteristics of God. During the retreat, I experienced them both. A far cry from the stern, judgmental, uncaring, drop-the-hammer kind of God I had been following. During what was called a cross ceremony, where we were given opportunities to nail our sins to the cross and have our feet washed by someone portraying Jesus, forgiveness became real to me. For the first time, I knew God had already forgiven me and my brokenness. It was not just a desire or hope. Now I knew the choice to walk in this forgiveness was a daily choice for me to make. There was another ceremony where we were invited to try on a robe, ring, and sandals. The same items the father supplied to the prodigal son in Luke 15 when he returned home after his time in the far country. I was part of his family. His son.

Following the retreat, I met with Chris again, and he inquired about the retreat. I was still on the mountaintop, excited and full of insight. I regurgitated the many things and experiences I grasped at the retreat. After my rambling had ceased, Chris responded in his usual soft tone, "That's great; I can see you going back again." I immediately thought, "How slow does he think I am, or what did I miss that was so big to send me back?"

I discovered the answer months later when I received a phone call at the control tower from a minister named Joe Donaldson, who later became the best friend I had and will ever have. Joe had heard about my experience and story at the last retreat and invited me to help serve on the next fall retreat. When Chris said I would go back, the last thing that crossed my mind was to go back and serve on the retreat. Since this conversation, I have learned another characteristic about God. He has a grand sense of humor. I will share more about the retreat and how it influenced my faith journey in later chapters, but from 2002 until 2020, I have been involved with every Faces of Christ retreat in some capacity.

God has put many people in my life who have helped me in my journey of experiencing and knowing Him. Four in particular stand out, though: my loving wife Joy, Chris Wood and his wise counsel, John Henderson who was my first real friend who cared about my soul more than my abilities, and Joe Donaldson, my best friend and mentor. Joy showed me what love really is, which helped me to see how God could love a ragamuffin like me. Chris patiently helped me to discover the wounds I live with and helped me begin to know Bob, the little boy whose Father in Heaven dearly loves him. John spent many nights fishing on the lake with me, sharing our hearts, failures, and fears with each other. Joe walks with me in life, encouraging, challenging, and even confronting me as he helps me to get a clearer understanding of this life and the great God we get to call Father. I will always cherish each of you from the depths of my heart.

Reflection Questions

1. Have you experienced a time in your life when you were filled with hope? Share the experience that initiated the hope you have and whether you are still living it.

2. Do you question whether you are loved and accepted by God? How does this affect your daily life?

3. How do you currently view God? What faces do you see Him wearing?

Part 2

Lessons from the Basement

Chapter 10

The Iceberg That Helped Save My Life

The story of the great ocean liner named the Titanic has been retold many times in literature and movies. It was touted as the most luxurious and safest ocean liner built in its time. Some even claimed it was unsinkable. Many of the most distinguished people of the day boarded the great ship for its maiden voyage on April 10, 1912 from Southampton, England to New York City.

Just five days later, as it traveled through the night while crossing the Atlantic en route to New York, the great ship struck an iceberg that ruptured its hull and caused it to sink. It is believed that of the approximately 2,200 passengers on board, about 1,500 of those perished in the icy waters. As the

The Iceberg That Helped Save My Life

ship sank on that frigid night, an iceberg had also taken down one of man's greatest accomplishments.

In the spring of 2002, I ran into a different type of iceberg. It wasn't one causing destruction — instead, it would help lift me up from the depths of my hopeless life that was heading for death. That might sound like a bold statement, but please allow me to explain. While attending the Faces of Christ retreat that my counselor Chris had encouraged me to go to, the leader began drawing a picture on a white board and asked the group if they could guess what it was.

After we all agreed it was an iceberg, he then added words beside the drawing and began to talk about what he had just written in relation to the iceberg.

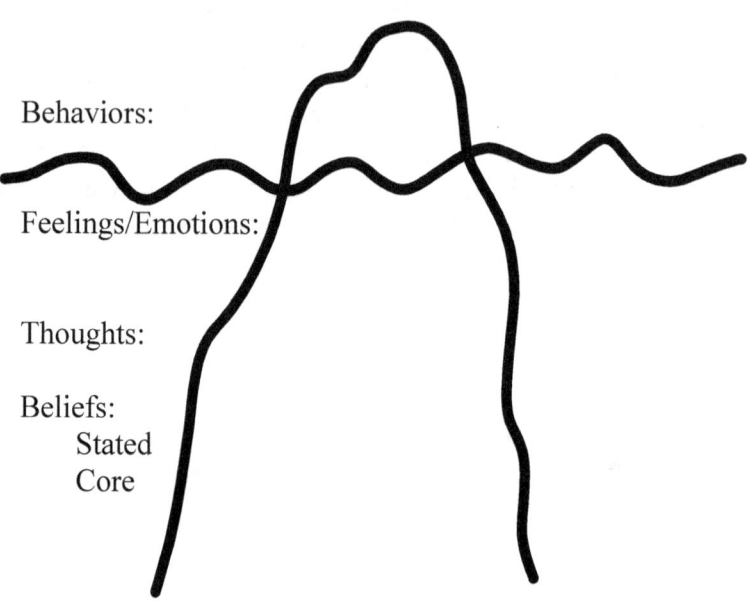

Layer 1: Behaviors

The leader began by asking what percentage of an iceberg is above the water and visible. One person responded with 10 percent, another 11. Most people would agree that somewhere in that range would be an average iceberg's exposure out of the water.

With the idea of using the iceberg to help understand ourselves and our actions, we began to talk about our **behaviors** that are most often visible to those around us. We tend to focus on the negative behaviors that people around us experience. Behaviors like addictions, anger, gossip, critical talk, and the like. It is also at the behavior level where we most often put our emphasis on stopping something negative in our life.

If we are honest with ourselves, all of us have something we struggle with and probably want to cease. Many of us have spent years of our lives trying to stop a behavior we know is against God's will for us. The constant failures lead us to a guilt- and shame-ridden life. I have thrown away countless computer discs and magazines that had improper images on them, thinking the lack of access to such would cure me. I have a filter installed on my computer to limit what I can view. My wife has been on multiple diets in her life. Sure, these attempts may succeed for a period, but if it is our "Signature Sin," as Christian author John Ortberg calls it in his book *The Me I Want to Be: Becoming God's Best Version of You*, we will eventually return to that behavior. Not that boundaries are bad things. They are certainly good steps toward success. The reality is that the root cause, the motivation in our core that directs us to seek the behavior, still exists.

We then attend church, and the sermon confronts us about a behavior we cannot control. During the sermon, at some point, the minister tells us we are not acting in accordance with God's will, and we need to repent and stop the behavior. Again, true statements. We know this, we even agree with the minister, and yet we are unable to stop. We promise ourselves one more time that we will try harder, and yet again, we rely on our willpower to control something we only understand at the surface level, the top 10 percent of the iceberg. So where do these habits and addictions come from?

Layer 2: Feelings and Emotions

The retreat leader went on to talk about the next layer of the iceberg — what was usually just below the surface. He labeled these our **feelings** or **emotions**. He said these are often somewhat hidden and are often triggers for our behaviors. In his book *The Voice of the Heart: A Call to Full Living*, Christian counselor Chip Dodd talks about how we misuse our feelings. Dodd says that we have eight true feelings: hurt, loneliness, sadness, fear, anger, shame, guilt, and gladness. Dodd states that while there are many more words that we express as feelings, like love and depression, and while they have feeling in them, they are much more than a feeling. They are conditions of the heart.

He goes on to say that all eight feelings are good because they are gifts from God. It is how we behave in response to these feelings that often causes sin in our lives.

For people pleasers like myself, we often stuff our feelings deep down, until one day we cannot contain them anymore. Then, we often explode in front of everyone around us. Picture trying to hold a beach ball under water — when you can't hold it anymore, it pops up with a splash.

I was very careful about not letting my feelings be known. At times, I did it so well that even I was not aware of what was going on inside me. Prior to the age of 42, I remember crying once in my life. I deeply loved my father-in-law. It would not be clear to me until years after his passing of a massive heart attack just how much. The night he passed, I sat at the foot of our bed with Joy at my side and sobbed uncontrollably for an extended time. Eventually, the sobs subsided, and I got up, washed my face, and did not cry again for 16 years.

Many times, while sitting in Chris's office during a session, he would ask me what I had felt or was feeling about a particular subject we were discussing. My response would be, "I don't feel anything." I had built such a fortress around my heart that I could not hear the voice inside. Later, Chris would help me begin to tear down that fortress, and the tears began to flow. I began to experience feelings that had not been possible before. I began to realize that my poor behaviors were connected to my lack of feelings. As this became clearer to me, Chris was ready to help me take the next step in my self-discovery journey.

Layer 3: Thoughts

The retreat leader began to share the next layer of the iceberg. He identified it as our **thoughts**. They are even more hidden than our emotions, unless you are the one that drives the rest of us batty by verbalizing everything that comes to mind. As I reflected back on recurring thoughts that flowed through my life, they always were negative. I would tell myself things like:

"No one cares about me."

"I will never do _____ to satisfy them."

"God can't love me, or He would stop me from doing _____."

"The world would be better if I wasn't here, so I should just end my life."

When using the iceberg as a tool, it is important to focus on thoughts that are reflecting what we are thinking about ourselves, and not on someone or something else. Yes, they may be a part of the thought, but we need to focus on what the thought is saying about us. For example, instead of "She never pays attention to me," say, "I don't feel loved in my marriage." By relating our thoughts to ourselves, it prepares us for the next level of the iceberg.

Chris would often question my thoughts and helped me to see the negativity in them. He helped me to see how often I used the words "should have," and encouraged me to begin using fewer condemning words like "could have." It is amazing how other people can see things in us that we are so blind to.

Layer 4: Beliefs

The last and deepest level of the iceberg that the retreat leader labeled is our beliefs. He broke down our beliefs into two categories. The first is our **stated beliefs**, which are what we say we believe at an intellectual level. The second is our **core beliefs**, which are deep within us and motivate us. These core beliefs are the most hidden in the iceberg, to the point that we often are clueless about their reality. In fact, we will often fight tooth and nail to prove we don't believe them because they can have such a sinful nature. That is exactly what I did.

This was probably the most challenging aspect of my counseling time with Chris. As he began to ask questions to help me begin to explore what Bob Head really believed about himself, it was at times like traveling through a black hole, because I could not or did not know the answers at my core. We repeatedly had to back up to the "behaviors" part of the iceberg, and drill down through the emotions and thoughts, until eventually the light bulb began to flicker.

Part of the challenge was that I was confusing my stated and core beliefs. I would state that God loves me, but in my heart did I really believe that. Another words, my stated belief was God loves me, but my core belief was I am not worthy of God's love. I would ask myself, "Do my thoughts, emotions, and behaviors line up with my stated beliefs?" The answer was always "no."

This led me one day, with Chris's help, to understand my core beliefs. While I believed that God loved me at an intellectual level – after all, I had accepted Christ as my Savior when I was 12 and had been a deacon at a church — that belief did not line up with the rest of the iceberg.

In my heart, my core belief was telling me that I was not worthy of being loved by God or anyone, after all that I had done. This complete lie from Satan had become my motivation for living. As crazy as it sounds, I believed God did love everyone around me, but there was no way He could love a broken person like me. Satan had taken me down the dark road of believing I was the only one who struggled with sexual sin, and therefore I was not loved. Chris had helped me go somewhere I do not think would have been possible on my own. The walls were too thick, and someone stronger than me needed to tear them down. I am so thankful that Chris allowed God to use him to do what I was not able to do. Now the question was, what could I do with this false belief, this lie, that had controlled my life?

* * *

When we use the iceberg as a tool to help us understand God and ourselves, we refer to it as "taking a trip to the basement." Again, beginning with behaviors, we walk down the steps of feelings and thoughts, and the last step is the most difficult. Many times, it requires a few half steps, if you will, before we step onto the basement floor or basement belief. My basement false belief was, "God does not love me."

Until I began to understand the motivation for my behaviors, I did not have a chance of overcoming them. None of the behavioral, emotive, and cognitive therapy I had tried throughout my life had lasting results. I needed some concrete reason why I would subject myself to such behaviors and sins before I could confront them. In other words, I needed to know what my enemy was and not just what it had manifested.

A few years ago, Joy and I were sharing our story with a group of marriage mentors, when God affirmed to me how much I had bought into Satan's ploy. While sharing with the group that I had believed I was the only one who struggled with sexual sin, God put a thought in my mind that flowed right out of my mouth: "I know I'm not the sharpest chisel in the toolbox, but I never thought to ask this question: 'Why did they publish so many *Playboys* for just one guy?'" That is how powerful my belief system had become. And yes, God and I had a good laugh over that one.

Here are some snapshots of how living with the false belief "I'm not worthy of being loved by God or anyone" played out in my life. As a child, when chaos filled our home, and the lie was taking hold, thoughts like, "Why doesn't my dad come to my football games?" or "Mom never tells me I do a good job at anything; she only corrects me when I mess up!" began to fill my mind. The feelings that would follow these thoughts were sadness, frustration, rejection, and loneliness. As the feelings intensified, I would dig out one of my magazines from its hiding place and go off alone to find solace. The behavior had started. I never felt rejection when looking at the images, and they always appeared perfect, as I wished the world could be. A perfect world where a father and mother showed love to their son, encouraged him, and spent time with him.

In my teenage years, life in the false belief would add more complexity. By now, my world had completely shattered. As I experienced promiscuous relationships that always ended in heartache, the pain and emptiness in my heart only grew worse. The list of people who did not love me kept growing. As a result, the desire to numb myself from the deep pain of this reality led me to alcohol and marijuana. Abusing these things allowed me to escape the pain I felt for a period of time, but there was always tomorrow. And the pain always returned.

As an adult, walking in the false belief added even more challenges to my life. I eventually learned that substance abuse did not really help, but actually magnified the pain I felt when the numbing wore off. Leaving the substance abuse behind was easier than I anticipated. However, as Joy and I became new parents and Joy was focusing on our baby daughter, I felt more alone and unloved. I would try to hide from this by having two careers and working long hours. Owning the woodworking business also added another benefit. It afforded the people pleaser in me an opportunity to earn love by pleasing people with my furniture. Looking back, it was truly an exhausting experience.

My sex addiction would always follow me through my loneliness. By the time I reached my adult years, computers and the internet would allow me to escape the pain of the day much easier than before. I could spend hours behind the computer trying to redefine love. And if that were not enough, having an affair would surely help me feel loved. That time in my life was the loneliest, most hopeless, and most unloved I ever felt. The very things I was hoping would help me to feel and be loved left me desolate and ready to end my life.

As the clarity of my false belief became more evident to me, I also realized it played out in all areas of my life. It was easy to grasp how porn and an affair might explain the false belief of not being loved. The porn was my attempt to feel loved, and the affair was my attempt to be loved. Becoming a people pleaser, I learned, was another response to the lie that was so prevalent in my life. The word "no" was not in my vocabulary, whether it was taking on more woodworking jobs, helping people fix things that I did not really have time for, or helping out the church when they asked for something. When asked to become a deacon at a church where we were members, I immediately responded with a "yes" as usual. There was no praying to seek God's will for my life behind any of it. It was simply Bob's people-pleasing attempts to earn acceptance and love. I lived in a state of tiredness and frustration that was always followed by resentment.

There are also two sides to the iceberg: If the left side is living with a false belief, guided by the world and Satan, the right side is living in God's spirit and being led by Him. It is walking in the belief of who God says He is and who He says we are; it is walking in the truth of His word.

In other words, instead of believing that I am not worthy of being loved, I began to replace that lie with God's truth — that through Jesus Christ, I am a child of God and dearly loved by Him. It becomes a selfless living and flows out of God's love for us. It is through His grace and His sacrifice of

His only son Jesus that our sins are forgiven and we are called His children. There is nothing I have done or could do to earn His love. I only had to accept His free gift and surrender my will to Him.

I learned a very valuable lesson when the desire to walk in God's truth became my life. At first, I focused mostly on my actions, living Christ-like behaviors, hoping they would lead me to healthier emotions, and creating Godly thoughts. Somewhat like a fake it till you make it mentality. I was just not able to make this work. Again, I was leaving God out of the equation and relying upon my own power and ability. Don't get me wrong — there are definitely behaviors that needed to stop immediately. I am speaking more in terms of a daily walk in God's truth.

As I again reflected on the iceberg model, I realized it was the focus (even though it became a subconscious focus) on the false belief that led to the life I had. I had not awoken one day and decided to become a sex addict. It was the focus on my false belief system that led to inaccurate thinking, unhealthy emotions, and destructive behaviors. With that knowledge, I began to focus on God's truth. Who He claims to be and whom He says I am. The focus on His truths began to lead me out of the basement with accurate thinking, which led to healthy emotions, followed by Godly behaviors.

I am still being changed and healed, as is my marriage. I expect this to occur the remaining days of my life on earth.

One other important reality I have learned: Each day when I wake up, and throughout the day, I get to make a choice. No one makes this choice but me. The choice is: Will I believe the lie and walk in death, or will I believe the truth of God and walk in freedom? It is my choice. I choose what belief system I will walk in.

Reflection Questions

1. Have certain emotions controlled how you walk through life? Which emotion is strongest for you, and why do you think it is so powerful?

2. Do you ever question where the motivations for your behaviors or addictions come from? Share some thoughts on possible origins.

3. Is there a false belief that has dictated how you live life? What impact does it have?

Chapter 11

A Night on the Lake

One of the characteristics of an addict is their desire to isolate. They keep people at an arm's length, fearing that they may be found out. That includes their spouse, children, family, and those they call friends. I spent 42 years in this state of isolation.

Isolation became one of the rules I lived by. Guard your heart from those around you because if they really knew you, they would hate you and not want to associate with you. And that would be very painful. I actually learned this rule as a young boy. We never invited friends to our home to play. I would go to their homes, play with their toys, and eat the chocolate chip cookies their mothers had made. However, as a family, we never reciprocated. Oh, they might make it to the front yard, but that was as close as they got. You see, we could not take the chance of chaos happening in our home when one of my friends was there. What would everyone think? Of course, you can guess who gets hurt the most through the act of isolation. I believe it to be the one doing the isolating. Undoubtedly, the people around them, the ones they love, are wounded as well by being ignored, unloved, and never getting to know the person next to them because of the isolation. But for the isolator, it becomes a self-fulfilling prophecy. For me, I believed at my very core that I was unworthy of anyone's love. (As I said before, I did not discover this until my 42nd year.) And yet I desperately wanted to be loved. Nevertheless, by isolating myself from others and God, I was not even giving them a chance to love me. What a sad existence.

Yes, there would always be a possibility of rejection. It was that fear of rejection that kept me enslaved for most of my life. I had a very strong work ethic. I worked extremely hard at whatever task was at hand to accomplish it in an efficient and correct manner. In reality, I worked in a very unhealthy way, working hard and long hours in hopes that rejection would not follow. I was a great employee and a great man to have around the home when things broke. Some would say I was a good friend to have around, especially when they had car troubles.

As He always does, God eventually confronted me about my fear of rejection. At the lowest point in my life, when I was ready to give up on myself, He stepped in. He began to show me love in very tangible ways. He would also help me understand that some people may reject me, but that should not be what I base my identity on. My identity was being His son. One who is dearly loved.

One day a few years back, Joy and I were carrying a very busy schedule. We were involved in too many things at

A Night on the Lake

church, watching our grandson while our daughter and son-in-law worked, and helping my dad care for my elderly mom. It was one of those times in which I struggled with believing the truth, and my false belief tried to make its way back in. As I mature in the faith, I am much quicker to run to the source of truth for help, but the doubt can still try to work its way in.

Joy was leaving our home to drive to Bardstown for a biweekly Bible study she was in, and I was heading to Home Depot to pick up some parts for a project I was working on. While driving, I began explaining to God that I was feeling unloved and asked Him to help me believe His truth and His love for me. After parking the truck and walking into Home Depot, I kept my head down, so as not to make eye contact with anyone. Looking back, I realize I had gone in to addict mode once again. Walking straight to the aisle where the parts were located, I collected what I needed and marched to the self-checkout counter, again to avoid any possibility of engaging with another individual. I scanned all the items and made the necessary payment. I did not even notice that behind me was the employee station that monitors the self-checkout area, or the employee who was at the station.

As I turned to leave, the employee I had not noticed was also turning to help a customer. As we both turned, not knowing each other's location, we came face to face within two feet from each other. As we were about to collide, we both stopped, and he asked, "How are you doing today?" I softly responded, "Not very well, actually." It surprised me that I spoke the truth of what I was feeling to a stranger. He then replied, "Well, I hope your day gets a lot better!" With that, he gave me the biggest sideways bear hug I had ever received. I responded with a broken, "Thank you." I walked out of Home Depot weeping like the 57-year-old little boy I was. Looking back, I remember seeing this employee many times during my trips to Home Depot. At most, we had a wave or a simple "hello" greeting. As I walked to my truck, I began to thank God for affirming His love for me. Some might doubt it, but for me, it was one tangible way God expressed His love for me.

Oh yes, I want to share about a night on the lake fishing with a friend, too. As I was learning the cost of isolation, God began to confront my way of relating to others. I had grown up knowing many men whom I called friends. They were men I worked with, fished with, played sports with, and partied with. Our conversations were always limited to the activities we shared. That is, what happened at work on a given day, what fishing lure was on the end of my rod, and whose party we were going to that night. In other words, we engaged in surface talk.

God was teaching me that there is more to friendship than what had passed for it in my life. At the recommendation of Chris, I reached out to our men's ministry, which in turn connected me to an accountability group. Week after week, our group would meet and talk about life and the journeys we walked. That in itself was really stretching for me, and yet there was more to come. John, one of the men in the group, and I really connected. And we began spending more time together and chatting more during the week. We worked on home projects together, went on weekend retreats at a local monastery, and enjoyed fishing in my boat. During these times, we would talk about God and our lives, but we were still somewhat guarded.

One night while bass fishing on Patoka Lake, the conversation John and I were having began to reach a much deeper level. It was one of those very clear evenings during a new moon phase, which made it very dark in spite of the

A Night on the Lake

beautiful stars shining above. So dark, that sitting in the back of my 16-foot bass boat, I could only see John's shadow in the front of the boat as he was casting.

We had been fishing for a few hours, having a great time and having our usual conversations. At one point, John said, "Bob, I have something I need to tell you, and you probably won't want to be my friend after that." At first, I was not sure how to respond. And what could it be? I had never heard such a statement before. Then suddenly I just blurted out, "When you are finished, I have some things I need to share with you also, and you won't want to be my friend either." What followed were two men sharing their deepest challenges and hearts with each other for one and a half hours. We both talked about our fears, failures, and struggles. I had never experienced a conversation like that before, with the exception of the recent conversations I had with my wife and Chris during my counseling sessions.

This began a new way of life for me when it came to relating with people. I wanted to really be known and really know those around me. I reached out to a few men I had recently met at church and began meeting and communicating with them weekly. Eighteen years later, three of those men and I meet weekly at different times. These connections help me from isolating, and these guys challenge and encourage me. As men, we are often loners and isolators by nature. Satan uses this to edge his way into our hearts. I know this is true from my experience and the experiences of the many men I have had the opportunity of counseling and mentoring.

A few years ago, this fact was laying heavy on my heart as I was walking with a few men that were being taken down by Satan's lies. I happened to be reading a book titled *Samson and the Pirate Monks: Calling Men to Authentic*

Brotherhood, written by Nate Larkin. In the book, Nate shares his story of living an isolated and loner lifestyle that took him down a dark, destructive path. After his family discovered the sin he had been hiding, he then shares his journey of healing and God's redemption in his life. Spending some time in 12-step programs, Nate realized there were two things missing for him in the programs. Instead of focusing on a behavior, Nate desired a group that was focusing on God and what He was doing in their lives. Not to forget or ignore the struggles or addictions we have, but to recognize the growth we experience as God walks with us through these things. Secondly, Nate desired a discipleship aspect to the group, where men were not just accountable to their sponsor but actually journeyed together through life, whether that is sharing dinner as a group after a meeting or talking throughout the week. As Nate and a few friends worked through these two desires, they formed the Samson Society groups. There are groups meeting worldwide, in many languages, along with virtual meetings happening throughout the week.

After reading Nate's book, God convicted me to begin a group in my home church. Joe Donaldson and I met Nate at the Frothy Monkey coffee shop in Franklin, Tennessee to discuss our idea and to gather further insights into the groups. A month or so later, after talking to Chris and another minister at my church, Joe and I formed our group. Every Wednesday evening, a group of diverse men gathers to talk about our challenges, struggles, and doubts about God. We also share victories that God has walked us through as He grows us. A common statement I hear from men is how the group is helping bring them away from the isolation they have been living in. We cannot and were not meant to walk through life alone.

A Night on the Lake

On September 25, 2012, I was sitting in the maternity waiting room of Norton Hospital awaiting the birth of our first grandchild. Joy and Nate (my son-in-law) were in the delivery room, comforting and encouraging Jenny through the birthing process. Together with Nate's and my family, we were anxiously awaiting the announcement. After a few hours in the waiting room, we began to receive pictures of the newborn that Nate was sending to his sister's phone. As we all gathered around her phone, we gazed with excitement at the pictures of my new grandson, taken just seconds after his birth. One picture showed him covered with the afterbirth fluid still dripping from him. Another picture highlighted the umbilical cord still connected and wrapped over his body. All of the pictures revealed his cone-shaped head that reminded me of what an alien might look like.

Have you ever thought of something, and while still thinking it, suddenly began to blurt it out? And once it exits your mouth, you wish you could take it back? That is exactly what happened to me that day in the waiting room. I suddenly blurted out, "Why are babies so ugly?" With that, the whole group admonished me to the other side of the room for a time out. Alone. After an hour or so of isolation, my phone rang, and when I answered it, a voice said, "Dad, do you want to come see your grandson?" At that, I jumped up from my time-out position, smirking as I walked past my discipliners, and headed for the delivery room.

I do not know what all they did in those 50 or so minutes from the time Logan was born, but when I saw him cleaned up and wrapped in a blanket lying beside his mom, with his dad kneeling beside him, I remember thinking it was one of the most beautiful sights I had ever seen. Logan was beautiful. They were beautiful together.

I began to think of something else while staring at this beautiful baby boy. He was totally helpless. Totally. He desperately needed his mom and dad for basic survival. He was not capable of living life on his own. He did not have the knowledge or ability to make it through the day. Not now, not ever. Whether it is the basics of life as a baby, or the companionship and encouragement needed as we grow into adulthood, we will always need people.

As I left the room after being blessed with witnessing the miracle of life, God reminded me that I was just like that little baby boy. I cannot live life alone either. I will always need Him and the people He puts in my life to challenge me and give me strength, encouragement, and love. I need it. We all need it. And He promised that He would always be there for me.

Reflection Questions

1. How would you describe your conversations with your friends? Are they focused on the news, weather, and sports, or do they go to the heart level?

2. Does the fear of rejection keep you from being vulnerable with others? If so, describe the effect it has on your relationships.

3. Are you a loner, living an isolated existence? What other reasons keep you from connecting with others.

Chapter 12

Stepping off the Cliff

A few years ago, my friend Joe and I went on a camping trip. Joe was putting together a father/son rite of passage retreat that he would lead for families at our church, as their sons became teenagers. It would consist of a few dads and their sons camping in the woods and include specific adventures for them to experience together. An opportunity for the dads to welcome their sons into the beginning of manhood.

One of the adventures Joe wanted to include was a time for rock climbing and rappelling. He and I were looking for a spot for this to take place, with a satisfactory camping area. We wanted to create an experience that wasn't too dangerous — but at the same time that wasn't so easy that the dads and sons would feel like they didn't accomplish anything. Leaving Louisville, we headed south, stopping at a few spots along the way, none if which met our expectations. We eventually landed in central Tennessee near the Great Stone Door area and located a very promising spot.

We began by checking out different areas where the group could rock climb. To know for sure, we would need to test these areas ourselves. Rock climbing would be our first adventure. Having never done either rock climbing or rappelling myself, Joe laid out the instructions for both. He connected me to the climbing rope, and up I went, with Joe coaching me along the way. I enjoyed climbing from the very beginning. Always planning my next move and focusing on my foot and hand placement never allowed me to think about how high I was climbing. It may have been a beginner's climb, but when I reached the top, I was shocked at how far I was from where I started.

Rappelling was a different story. We located a rock wall Joe felt would be a good height for beginners. Joe tied the rope around a very large oak tree at the top of the rock wall. He offered to go first to illustrate the technique. I quickly obliged. He strapped on the harness, backed up to the edge of the wall, and just stepped off. Peering over the cliff, I saw him dangling in the air as he "walked" down the rock wall. All the way down, he was telling me how great the views were. After reaching the bottom, Joe began the long walk up the trail to reach the top of the cliff where I was waiting.

It was now my turn. He gave me some further instruction on how to navigate the wall and then strapped the harness on me and threaded the rope. Now it was time for my part. I thought it was a simple thing, really. Just back up to the edge of the cliff, lean back, and let go, if you will — not of the rope, of course, but of everything in my head telling me this cannot be right. I backed up to the edge, looked down at the bottom where I was to land, and just froze. I could not take the next necessary step to experience rappelling.

Joe, sensing my fear, offered to demonstrate the technique one more time. I quickly walked from the edge, disconnected the rope and harness, and helped him get back into the harness. Like the first time, Joe just backed up to the cliff, stepped off, and disappeared. Now, even more, I wanted to experience the thrill of rappelling. Again, Joe made his way up the trail and asked if I would like to give it a shot. Everything in me wanted to back off the cliff, and yet everything in me was also full of fear and doubt. "What if?" has always been a big part of my life. The fear that comes with it has either controlled me or limited me from experiencing much of what life had to offer. This time would be different.

For the second attempt, Joe helped me step into the harness and rope and then reiterated the instructions for rappelling. I backed up to the edge, looked down at my landing spot…and froze. Joe, again sensing my reluctance said, "Bob, you don't have to do this. I will not think any less of you if you choose not to do it. Many people are unable to take the step over the edge." I responded rather meekly, "I want to do this. I need to do this."

A few seconds later, which seemed like forever, I backed off the cliff. I took that next step. The step that had to happen for me to experience rappelling. The step that would allow me to face a fear that had been keeping me from experiencing more out of life. A step that would allow me to confront a doubt I believed. And there I was, with a grin on my face, hanging off the side of the rock wall. It was maybe the freest I ever felt in life. The light wind was causing me to drift from side to side, and I would kick off the smooth rock wall from time to time.

I let out a little more rope and descended down the wall. The further I went, the more I swayed. It was an amazing feeling, and the view around me was breathtaking, just as Joe had described. I was in no hurry to get to the bottom. At one point, I asked Joe to take some pictures of me hanging in midair. It took him awhile to traverse down the trail to where he could see me well enough to take a picture.

Eventually, I made it to the bottom of the wall, disconnected the rope, and made the trek back up the trail where Joe was waiting. I thanked him for the incredible experience and patience while I worked through my fears. I had done it! I experienced rappelling and did not allow my fears and doubts to stop me. That day, I chose to face them.

A few days later, I found myself lying in our tent in southern Kentucky, where we stopped as we made our way back home. As the heat from the early morning sun came through the tent, I began to reflect on the last few days, and in particular on our time of rappelling. I thanked God for giving me the courage to face the fear as I remembered asking for His help on the edge of the cliff. He then reminded me that the way I had approached backing off that cliff was the same way my walk of faith with Him had been.

As I stood on top of the rock wall, in my mind, there was no doubt the setup Joe had brought would work. The large oak tree Joe had tied the rope to was plenty strong to hold us, and probably could have held my house up, too. The rope was large and strong enough to hang my truck from with no problem. In addition, the harness had just supported Joe two times, and I did not weigh that much more than Joe did.

My relationship with God was much like my rappelling experience. Intellectually, I knew God loved me. I had read my Bible through many times since I was 12 years old. I remembered the verses that say that God is love, and that God loves all His children. I had heard many sermons in my life telling about His love. Yet my fears and doubts kept me stuck at the intellectual level of belief. Something was missing.

Then, God reminded me what had happened when I tried rappelling a second time. I surrendered my fears and doubts and focused on the facts so I could experience the thrill. Then, I simply stepped off the cliff. Only then did I truly know and experience the truth that the rappelling system would support me and that it was safe. Not just for Joe. Not just for everyone else. But for me, too.

God helped me to see that a few years earlier, my faith in him had taken a similar step off a cliff. It was definitely a weak faith, but it was faith nevertheless. It was all I had. The night I lay on my bedroom floor when Joy found out about the affair, I finally began to surrender my fears and doubts about God. As I gave my fears and doubts to Him to deal with, I began to experience and know Him. Not just to know about Him and what I had read about Him. It became personal. I began to experience His truth, His strength, His support, and His love. But not until I surrendered my truth, my strength, my will, and my ideas of love could this happen. He had been patiently waiting years for me to take that one step of surrender that was keeping me from knowing and experiencing Him in the deepest parts of me. My Father in Heaven who desperately loves me and desires to walk with me daily waited for me to let go.

To be honest, I have surrendered many times since that night on my bedroom floor. To be more accurate, my choice to surrender is a daily one. I have learned that Satan does not give up on us just because we surrender one time. He uses people and life circumstances to try to reintroduce those fears and doubts that we have turned over to God. Maybe that is why the Christian life is often called a life of surrender. Daily, we have opportunities to choose to surrender to God or pick up again our fears and beliefs that are detrimental to us. We can be frustrated that the evil one continually attacks us and our sinful nature, or we can allow God's grace to be the source that keeps us close to Him.

When I share my story with the men that I mentor, they will often ask, "But how do you know if you have surrendered or not? I think I have many times, but nothing really changes." It is not for me to judge whether they have surrendered. That is between them and God. I have learned some things about what surrender looks like in my life.

First, most of us do not truly surrender if we think we still have a chance of working things out. It does not matter if it is an addiction, a disease, job loss, or loss of a marriage. Our egos and pride are just too big. Some do not trust God enough to hand over their challenges. And our bottoms are all different. Each of us arrives at the end of our rope at different places because our ropes are different lengths. The end of me, Bob, came only when feeling my only worldly choice left was to end my life. I have met other men who acknowledged the end of their rope came with a job loss or threat of divorce, or even from years of living in solitude. I have also met those that have not arrived at their bottom and continue to struggle through life. However, we might agree that God patiently waits for us. He is a gentleman and does not force His way into our life. Even though we often wish He would.

Secondly, I believe we sometimes confuse surrendering to God with giving up something we really did not want anymore, and that did not have the grip on us like some things. For me, it was alcohol and marijuana. Giving these two up led me to believe I was surrendering my life to Christ. I understand these may be the strongholds for someone else, but they were not my kryptonite. Eventually, I came to understand they were only numbing mechanisms that I had been using. It was really my sexual addiction and false beliefs that God was waiting for me to surrender to Him. These were what had been keeping me from connecting with God on an intimate level.

Often, when we do surrender, we do so that we might get something in return. Yes, God promises much to the surrendered heart, but our motivation still can involve our ego. Many times, I had the thought that if I could surrender my addiction to porn, God would actually like and love me. That thought alone was my way of manipulating God's love by using the if-then equation. The reality was that God already loved me. My pride in wanting something blinded me to the truth. There is nothing I can do or not do that will make God love me more or less. He just does. There is still more surrendering for me to do in this area, and yet God still welcomes me with open arms. Much like He did with the prodigal son in Luke 15.

Finally, I think we have to ask ourselves, do we really even want to lead a surrendered life? Am I willing to let go of my pride and will? We often say that we are, but our lives do not reflect it. Our behaviors, emotions, thoughts, and beliefs remain on the left side or false belief side of the iceberg. In reality, we are still fooling ourselves. Jeremiah 29:13 addresses this very issue when it states, "You will seek me and find me when you seek me with all your heart." We find and experience God when we surrender all of our lives to Him and not just the things that are easy for us to let go.

Do we really want to live a surrendered life?

Reflection Questions

1. Where would you rate your level of faith on a scale of 1-10, with 10 being the highest? Would you say your faith was more an intellectual faith or a faith from your heart?

2. Have you ever had a time in your life when God invited you to step off a cliff so that He could grow your faith and trust in Him? If so, what was your response?

3. Have you experienced true surrender to God in your life? If so, what were the circumstances?

4. Do you believe surrender is a choice to make over and over in life?

Chapter 13

All About Change

My friend Jerry and I have been meeting on Thursday mornings for several years. We are an unlikely pair, but it works. In many ways, we are polar opposites. Jerry used to read law books for fun and became a lawyer. I read how-to books and became a woodworker. Jerry is a very black and white person in his ways of thinking, and I am always looking for some grey areas. Jerry is a matter-of-fact truth teller, and I am all about giving people grace. Our relationship, as different as it is, has allowed God to use each of us to help the other become more Christ-like. God is using our differences to help us grow. One week, it may be Jerry helping me to see where I am short on truth, and the next week it may be me helping Jerry see where grace might be needed in a situation he is going through. We have embraced our differences, and God continues to work through both of us.

One Thursday, I was sharing with Jerry about a couple Joy and I had been mentoring, leaving out their identities as to not break confidentiality. The challenges they were up against, the unwillingness to change or show grace to each other. They said they wanted a better marriage and relationship with God, but their actions were not aligning with that.

After a few minutes of sharing my frustration about the couple, Jerry stopped me and calmly said, "Bob, people are living the life they want to live."

"Huh?" I responded.

Again, he said, "People are living the life they want to live."

I rebutted with, "But how can that be? They are seeking help through mentoring; they share with us their challenges and the things they want to change. Seems to me they are not living the life they want."

As we discussed this idea further, Jerry asked me if I saw anything they were doing differently that would help their lives to change. Were they taking to heart the things we were asking of them? Was there any evidence they were turning over to God the challenges they were facing? The answer to these questions, of course, was an emphatic "no."

So why do we say we want to change and then do not exert the effort to make it happen? Why do we continue to live the life we say we do not want to? Why did I live 42 years in a life so miserable that I was willing to destroy it rather than change it for the better?

To begin with, many of us are afraid of change. Change can be very hard. It takes us out of our comfort zone, even if our comfort is not very comfortable. That also makes change scary. As we give away control so that change will happen, we also give up our way of life and what we know.

On the Faces of Christ retreat, we began with an exercise called the change exercise. Everyone partnered up, and the leader asked us to face each other no more than two feet apart and observe each other closely. This activity tends to create some very awkward moments, which is not part of our daily lives. How often do we stand inches from someone other than our spouse and intently look him or her over? The instructor then told us to turn back to back and change five things about our appearance. After this, we faced each other again and tried to identify each other's changes. We then repeated the exercise, changing five more things about ourselves. By this time, people started to look ridiculous. To finish, the instructor asked us to change seven more things about ourselves. At that, the grumbling started, and the exercise ended.

We then began to discuss seven things about change, many of which we unknowingly used in the exercise.

Lesson 1: We Don't Like Change

The first thing we discussed is how we do not usually like change, especially change we do not choose. Most of us struggle with being told what to do, even if we think it is a good thing. Our pride always tells us something different. I have heard men say to me, "My wife says I need to stop _____! And I think she is being unreasonable." After asking him several questions about what his wife wants him to stop, the husband will respond, "I don't want to stop, and she can't tell me what to do." We do not like change, especially if it is not our own doing.

Lesson 2: We Focus on the Loss

Second, when it comes to change, we usually think of what we are going to lose. Chris and I talked about this in my counseling. One day, he warned me that there would be a grieving process to go through as I surrendered my porn addiction to God. He wanted me to be prepared for that journey, as I would be confronted with what I was losing. He was right. I missed the comfort it gave me when facing difficult times in my life. Nevertheless, eventually, I began to focus on the freedom and peace that came from a life free of porn. It was a hurdle for me to overcome.

Lesson 3: We Make Easy Changes First

Third, we tend to change the easy things first. It was easy for me to stop drinking and smoking marijuana. They did not have the power over me that porn did. Even a more difficult change, like cutting back as a workaholic, was possible with my wife's help. The people pleaser in me found it very difficult to say "no" to work, and I asked Joy to help me. We agreed that before I automatically said "yes" to someone, I would always begin by letting him or her know that Joy kept up with my calendar, and I would have to check with her first. She then would ask me the hard questions:

"Is this something you would really like to build?"

"Do you really have time to build this with what is already on your schedule?"

"Are you trying to get acceptance from someone?"

With Joy's help, cutting back on work became much easier. However, when it came to porn, it was much different. That change would seem impossible. The shame that came with it kept me from asking for help. My own willpower was never sufficient for the job. As a result, this change would never happen until I was ready to surrender all the feeble tools in my toolbox and allow the power of the Holy Spirit to do what only He could do.

Lesson 4: We Really Just Re-Arrange

Fourth, much of change is really re-arranging. During the second round of the change exercise, we changed the same things again. If the first change was taking a pen from my shirt pocket and placing it behind my ear, on the second round, I moved it to my front pants pocket. I have heard that many folks attending AA meetings, while they are sober, begin to smoke. I have also seen people give up smoking, but then they begin to gain weight. We move the pain of our brokenness from one addiction to another. The problem with this process is that we never address the deeper issue that motivates us to turn to addictions.

Lesson 5: We Stop Too Early

Fifth, after making some changes, we tend to think we've done enough, and we stop too soon. I remember thinking that if I could stop watching porn, God would really like me because I would be a decent person, and I would be done changing. That thinking was so wrong on many levels. The reality of it is we do not want to live a life of constant change. Yet God says that is exactly what the Christian walk looks like. If we are going to become Christ-like, we as humans have more than just one thing that needs to change in our lives. Often, our one big sin keeps us from seeing our many smaller sins.

Lesson 6: We Don't Ask for Help

Sixth, we do not expect or often ask for help from others when it comes to change. I will go further and say we often think people will not understand our issues, and if they did, they probably would distance themselves. This may be the most fear-driven of these aspects of change because it brings vulnerability to a deeper level. Letting someone know of our struggles is a very scary thing to do, especially when seeking to be loved and accepted is at the core of who we are. We fear rejection, and so to invite someone (including God) into our lives would be too big of a chance to take. I have found this thinking to be wrong. The very people who love me the most and know my sinfulness (including God) are the ones helping me navigate my journey. Yes, there are some people who are incapable of understanding and forgiving, but I am choosing to walk with those who know their brokenness and love me in spite of mine.

Lesson 7: We Return to Our Old Ways

Lastly, after a period of change, we often go back to where we started. Matthew 12:43-45 says, "When the unclean spirit has gone out of a person, it passes through waterless places seeking rest, but finds none. Then it says, 'I will return to my house from which I came.' And when it comes, it finds the house empty, swept, and put in order. Then it goes and brings with it seven other spirits more evil than itself, and they enter and dwell there, and the last state of that person is worse than the first." We often find ourselves returning to our old ways. But when we focus on God and His truth, our thoughts, feelings, and behaviors align with what is right.

That was certainly my way of life for 42 years. I would try to change some aspect of my addiction, throwing away magazines, reading my Bible more often, and deleting images from my computer, promising myself never to act out again. Yet after awhile, I would always go back, and each time, the draw became more powerful. Even though I tried to believe the truth of God — that He loved me as He loved everyone else — it never made it to my heart. As I tried to sweep myself clean of false beliefs and sinful behaviors, my guilt and shame would bring in more dirt than ever.

* * *

I think sometimes change does not happen because we have learned to accept or ignore our pain. The author Dr. Henry Cloud once said, "We change our behavior when the pain of staying the same becomes greater than the pain of changing. Consequences give us the pain that motivates us to change."

My dad struggled with alcohol and smoking for years. I remember many times when he would try to quit one or the other, but it never seemed to last. It wasn't until years later when us kids were grown and moved out that my mother finally had enough and kicked Dad out of the house. He came to my house and explained what was going on. I offered for him to come and work in the wood shop while he tried to figure things out. I encouraged him to contact his priest and share with him what he had been telling me, which he did. Dad had told me that the pain of losing his wife was far greater than letting go of the alcohol and cigarettes that were killing him and his marriage. Dad was finally ready to allow God to change his heart. Amazingly, he was able to quit both alcohol and smoking at the same time. Mom and he enjoyed another 30 or so years of a good marriage. Before Mom's passing, Dad and I were having lunch one day, and I thanked him for modeling for me how to love your wife in your senior years. He loved her well.

Chris encouraged me at times to talk to Dad about my childhood and how it had impacted me. He knew that I needed to do this for positive change in my life to continue. The relationship between my dad and me was improving, but it would take some time before I could have that conversation.

I began to pray to God that if this conversation with my dad were to happen, I needed Him to set it up. Sometimes I wish God didn't listen to all my prayers, because He did just that. Two days after I began praying, a few events happened in our lives that allowed Dad and me to begin talking. I was able to share my hurt and anger that I had toward him, and he listened intently. When I was finished, he apologized. He said that he wished things had been different, that he knew he couldn't change the past, but moving forward, he wanted to be a better father to me.

I know some will not have the opportunity that I had, as their dad may have passed or is still struggling, but there was one more thing God was leading me to do, and he leads us all to do — and that was for me to forgive my dad. Only then could our relationship go to the next level. Forgiving my father was followed by something even more difficult for me to do for change to continue. That was to forgive myself. And I did. I no longer wanted my hesitance to forgive myself to keep me in bondage, and I needed God's help for that to happen.

I cannot do change alone. There are times when I pray to God to help me believe His truth so I can continue on the journey of change. I need Joy and others around to help me become more solid in my walk. There is a saying in 12-step programs that goes like this: "It doesn't matter how far down the road you are; you are still right next to the ditch." I believe this is true for all of us. We all have some struggle, sin, or addiction that is always ready to hinder our journey with Christ. In the 15 years Joy and I have been walking with couples, we have yet to meet someone for whom this was not the case. Whether it is a desire for perfection (in our appearance or our home), gossip, or an addiction like drugs, sex, or food, our struggles keep us from an intimate relationship with Christ.

This is an important fact for us to remember. We are all susceptible to falling in the ditch because we are all walking right beside it. First Corinthians 10:12 reminds us of this fact when it says, "So, if you think you are standing firm, be careful that you don't fall!"

Next, we will look into how we can navigate our journeys while always being so close to the ditch.

Reflection Questions

1. Are there changes that you desire in your life, but haven't taken the steps required to make happen? Why not?

2. Which of the seven roadblocks resonate with you when it comes to change? Explain how.

3. What things in your life do you need help with changing? Who might you ask for help and why?

Chapter 14

The Well-Worn Path

You may call me a city boy. With the exception of four months or so, I have lived in the same city, Louisville, Kentucky, for 63 years.

I also grew up hiking, camping, backpacking, and appreciating the great outdoors. Since my high school years, I have spent many days exploring the Smoky Mountains area of the Appalachians. Now in my 60s, I still love hiking. But at the end of the day, I look forward to a nice, comfortable bed with a nice, comfortable pillow to lay my head on.

From time to time, my treks would intersect parts of the Appalachian Trail. This trail extends between Springer Mountain in Georgia and Mount Katahdin in Maine. In all, it is approximately 2,200 miles long and navigates through 14 states. It will typically take a hiker five to seven months to complete.

A friend of mine completed the 2,200-mile trek before starting college. He was a very focused person but would later acknowledge there were times when he would stray from the trail. Sometimes, he was drawn to the amazing scenery, and other times, he struggled to identify the trail. However, he always found his way back so that he could complete the trek. He talked of challenges along the way, including bear encounters, poor weather, areas with treacherous hiking conditions, and running low on food and water. Nevertheless, he regained focus and finished the long hike.

I, on the other hand, would be hiking and would sometimes unintentionally intersect with the trail and hike a small portion of it. Not because I was passionate about it, but just so I could say I had done it.

I think many of us live out our spiritual journeys in similar ways. God has taught me that my journey must be intentional. Much like my friend who completed the trail, I want to stay on my path. I want my focus to be on God so I know the direction He wants to take me. Yes, I will wander from the path from time to time, as my friend did while hiking. However, my focus on intentional living will always bring me back. Life with Christ leading the way is exciting, scary, exhilarating, and peaceful.

A few years ago, Joe and I went hiking in North Carolina. It was in an area of the Appalachian Mountains I had never seen before. As we were hiking, Joe explained that we were heading to an area called Max Patch. Max Patch is a bald mountain that peaks at about 4,600 feet. As you reach the summit, there is an absence of trees and an abundance of grasses. The views are spectacular.

As we walked along the mountain, we came upon an area where the Appalachian Trail joins it and continues some distance along its peak. As I looked over the trail, I was astonished to see how worn it had become. Not only was the vegetation absent, but hikers' use of the path had also created a ditch as far as I could see. The ditch was approximately 16 inches deep by 16 inches wide. So narrow I found it difficult to walk in. Nevertheless, countless hikers before me had done just that. It was such a well-worn path that was easy to follow.

As I reflected on what we saw on Max Patch, I began to think about the path in relation to my life and spiritual journey with God. Remembering the left side of the iceberg model, it began to make sense. Why did I keep doing the same behaviors repeatedly? Why did I feel the same emotions throughout my life? Moreover, why did those terrible thoughts about others and myself keep invading my mind? As I pondered these questions, I began to realize it all started with my belief system. I had begun hiking the path of false beliefs, the lies of Satan, at a very young age, and I had dug a narrow and deep ditch.

Then one day, the truth side of the iceberg, walking in God's truth, set me on a new path. As I continue on my journey, that new path is becoming clearer and easier to follow. This one is not like the disgusting one I had created on my own. Instead, it is a path that adds to the beauty of His creation while He does the work, as I continue to surrender.

To be honest, at first, I was reluctant to walk this new path. I was fearful, not knowing where I was going. At least my old path was known. I had to relinquish all control on the new path, where my old ways allowed me to be in control. In addition, I was fearful of what might be asked of me. My old path allowed me to choose what I would and would not do.

God began taking me places I never dreamed of going. He showed me how much better life was when I let go of the steering wheel and turned all navigation over to Him.

So what did this new path look like? God led me to places I would not have chosen on my own. One of the first adventures was God prodding me to share my story at the Faces of Christ retreat. I have always been afraid of speaking in front of people. In Sunday school, I would do my best to avoid being asked to read Bible verses. I literally would begin shaking, and my voice quavered. However, God was persistent in this. The first time I spoke at the retreat, I barely slept the week before. As I timidly got up from the table and walked to the podium, I said to God, "I need your help to get the words out." And together we got through it.

Since that first night of sharing, God has taken me to Alaska and other parts of the nation, as well as all the way to Kenya to share His story with groups of men. I am somewhat less fearful than I used to be, but I still need and ask for His help every time He leads me to the next group. I know that was His intention all along. To walk with me in life. And each time I follow Him in this new path, the less fear and uncertainty I feel. As the song says, "Where He leads me I will Follow."

There is one last thing to consider: Believing the truth of God and walking in His loving path is not a one-time choice, nor is it an easy choice. I have learned the world and Satan do not give up on me because one day I chose God.

Choosing the truth is a choice I get to make every day and many times throughout the day. There really are only two choices — either God's way, or my way. One will always win out, and I have to be intentional about which one I walk. There have been times of weakness in which I even ask God to help me choose Him. As His word says in 1 Corinthians

10:13, "No temptation has overtaken you except what is common to mankind. And God is faithful; He will not let you be tempted beyond what you can bear. But when you are tempted, He will also provide a way out so that you can endure it." Mother Teresa once responded to that verse by saying, "I know God won't give me anything I can't handle. I just wish He didn't trust me so much." When I choose His way out, as painful as life has gotten, He is always there to help me endure the pain.

Reflection Questions

1. What ways can you be more intentional about your spiritual journey? What is keeping you from choosing this path of intentionality?

2. Describe the path you have traveled so far in your journey of faith. Has it been the path of truth or the path of self-protection/self-satisfaction?

3. Do you fear walking in the path of truth knowing you won't have control, know the next step, or choose which direction? Why or why not?

Chapter 15

Guitar Lessons

Six years ago, I began building acoustic guitars. Today, I started construction of my 39th build. It has been an interesting journey from the beginning, and as usual, God has taught me many lessons through the process.

I have been playing guitar since my teenage years but never thought seriously about actually building one. I did briefly consider the idea 20 or so years ago, but after a little research, I concluded that by the time I built and bought all the equipment necessary to construct a guitar, the money invested would be better spent on a relatively expensive guitar. So I bought a Martin D28, and the short-lived idea of building a guitar was history.

That is until six years ago when I was in a different place. My life had slowed down, and I was able to devote time to something that would take an extended period to learn. Even then, building guitars was not on my radar until my friend Dean came to me one day and mentioned that we should try to build a few. I blurted out, "That's the silliest thing I've heard lately." I once again tabled the idea until later that year, when Joy gave me a book on building guitars for a Christmas present. Even as I unwrapped the book, I thought, "Why did she buy me this?"

And there was my first lesson. In my life, I have found if God wants me to do something, He is very persistent. He is also patient. He will use many ways to get His point across, from a seed planted 20 years prior, to people He has put in my life, to a wrapped present lying under a Christmas tree. Proverbs 16:9 says, "In their hearts humans plan their course, but the Lord establishes their steps." God was persistent in showing me what steps to take next in life.

With the book in hand, the journey began. My serial obsessive behavior kicked in, and I began reading anything I could get my hands on to help me understand the process of building acoustic guitars. With the advent of the internet, the amount of information available on the topic seemed limitless.

Three months after receiving the book for Christmas, the construction of the first guitar began. It was about that time that God was ready to teach me lesson number two.

One day, while working in the shop, things did not feel right with me. There was not anything physically wrong with me, but rather something deep within my soul that felt off. I was meeting my friend Tony for lunch in a few hours, so as usual, I pushed on with my day until lunchtime.

While catching up, Tony became very interested in my guitar building. As I was sharing with him about my journey, the light bulb came on, and God made it through my thick skull. I said to Tony, "In my obsessive focus on learning to build guitars, I have forgotten about everything else in my life, including God, my wife, and my family."

I had years ago come to understand how the many poor behaviors in my life had affected my relationship with God, but building guitars was not an inherently evil behavior. While sitting with Tony, God was affirming to me that any worldly thing I obsessed over would distance me from Him.

Tony then asked me, "Don't you think your Heavenly Father who created you and gave you these talents would want to sit with you in the shop and watch you build guitars?"

Without a thought, my quick response was, "No, why would He want to sit and watch me do something that He already knows I can do because He made me that way? Why would He want to waste His time like that? He has bigger things to do."

Tony sat in silence, as he could clearly see me pondering my response. Then, in broken speech with tears in my eyes, I responded to my own questions: "I think that way because my earthly father didn't take time to sit and watch me as I fixed or built things as a young boy." Please do not hear this as me blaming my dad or being a victim. Rather, I was projecting my view of my earthly father onto my Heavenly Father.

My Heavenly Father was letting me know He was not anything like my earthly father, and it was time to learn more about His true identity. Tony concluded the conversation by saying, "I think your Heavenly Father would like to be invited into your workshop and hang around while you build." That is exactly what I began to do. I began inviting God to join me, to sit with me, and to teach me. I would often ask, "What are we going to build today?" Once again, God was becoming my focus, which allowed everything else to be in its proper place. Jeremiah 29:13 says, "You will seek me and find me when you seek me with all your heart." That includes obsessing over guitar building. He was not telling me to quit building guitars, but that He wanted to be a part of that area of my heart also.

This brings me to the next lesson God taught me while building guitars: Sound is subjective because He has made us such unique individuals with different qualities and likes; a sound that one person enjoys, the next person may not. I can build a nice guitar with a given combination of woods that my ears love to hear, and yet someone else will bypass that guitar and pick another one with a different combination of woods; one that my ears find subpar in tone quality over the first guitar. This is helping me to let go of my need to people please and instead enjoy the process of using God's creation to build instruments.

I believe it is amazing that God used something as simple as guitar building to confront me at the very depths of my heart. Early on, the idea came to mind for me to honor God in a small way. As I built each guitar, I would inlay a mother of pearl cross on the headstock. The cross reminds me of all the materials He created to build beautiful-sounding guitars and the many lessons He taught me in the process – and I am sure there are many more to come. Maybe most of all, after some 39 guitars and hundreds of hours, it reminds me of all the times I have spent in the shop with my Heavenly Father working together and enjoying part of His creation.

Reflection Questions

1. Do you sense God leading you in a specific direction? Are you following, or is something keeping you stuck where you are?

2. Do you sometimes find yourself so busy or so focused on something that you forget about what is important in life, like God and family? What things in life take you there?

3. Sitting in God's creation has always brought me more intimacy with God. What things in life bring you to a closer relationship with your Heavenly Father? Are you making time for them?

Chapter 16

The Sinking Boat

If you were to Google "people's greatest fears in life," you would find quite a list. This list often includes a fear of public speaking, bugs, snakes, small spaces, heights, flying, and dying. By no means is this an exhaustive list. The point is we all have fears in our lives. Many of these fears we do not discuss with others because they often remain in our subconscious until a trigger brings them out. Other times, we do not share our fears because they have such control over us that we have acted in ways that have caused great shame and guilt.

Several years ago, when our daughter Jenny was approaching her teens, our family traveled with a group of Model A enthusiasts to a friend's farm for an outing. It was a beautiful, sunny summer afternoon. The farm had a small lake on it with a paddleboat sitting on the bank. After our picnic lunch with the group, my friend Emeric (who I had enjoyed working with on Model A's for many years) suggested that Jenny, he, and I try out the paddleboat. After getting the owner's approval, the three of us climbed aboard the small boat and began paddling around the lake. The water was calm and glistening.

About 15 minutes into our venture, Emeric suddenly began yelling indistinguishable words and proceeded to rise out of his seat. He then leaned backwards, apparently trying to get to the rear of the small boat. This sudden movement by Emeric caused the front end of the boat to rise out of the water and eventually flip the boat completely over while throwing us into the lake.

With no life jacket on, I began trying my best to swim to shore. As I was struggling to stay afloat, Jenny, being a great swimmer, decided to swim up from behind me and grab my neck. I began to wonder if either of us would make it to shore. As I was doing my best to keep Jenny and myself above water, I was also looking for Emeric to see where he ended up. Looking to my right, I saw Emeric about three feet away, laughing uncontrollably at what he was seeing. As he regained his composure, he yelled, "It is only about three feet deep, and I am standing on the bottom!"

At that, I stopped flailing and cautiously let my feet down until they reached the bottom of the pond, while Jenny still hung onto the back of my neck. After calming down, Emeric and I pulled the capsized boat back to shore. When the fear subsided, the whole group enjoyed a great laugh, as they had been watching the scene play out from the shore. The hosts found us some dry clothes, and we enjoyed the rest of the beautiful day.

Once back on shore, Emeric explained that he was deathly afraid of spiders. When one began to climb up the steering wheel he was holding, he lost it and reacted. The fear of

The Sinking Boat

spiders was not something he faced on a daily basis, and sharing it with me had never been necessary until that day.

I believe there was a greater fear at work inside me: Kakorrhaphiophobia.

Kakorrhaphiophobia is an abnormal, persistent, irrational fear of failure. It is debilitating and the most extreme version of what we think of the fear of failure. At times, we all face doubt, anxiety about our capabilities, and fear of what others think, but usually not at the debilitating level.

Unknowingly, I lived with this fear for 42 years. It was birthed by my deep desire to be loved and at the same time living in the belief that I was not worthy of such love. Fear of failure dictated my every move in life. Whether in my personal or professional life, it was always my guiding torch. My daily core question was: How can I make it through the day without failure?

My careers were never about amassing a large sum of money. Yes, I needed money as we all do to survive, and money at times was useful to help temporarily numb the pain that flowed through me. My goal was always to do something so people would notice me. Whether they admired my career choice or liked something I had created. When I felt I had failed, it was devastating.

As the failures mounted, usually in my mind only, it was not just that I had failed at something. Adding the sin of sexual addiction that I was unable to control to these imagined failures, being a failure became an even stronger part of my identity. Not only was I failing the people around me, but I was also failing God. Satan was having a field day with me.

This fear also limited my life and opportunities that came my way. I have always loved automobiles and auto racing. In particular, I enjoy stock car racing like NASCAR. I would watch the races on the television each week, wishing that one day I could drive a car like that in a race.

One day, while working at the control tower, I received a phone call from one of the employees at Standiford Field Airport. He knew how much I loved racing, and he had been racing at some local tracks around our town. He was ready to get out of racing and wanted to know if I was interested in buying his car.

I struggled with the idea of whether I could do that, not because of the money or time, but because I felt unworthy to own and race a car. The fears were running rampant as the idea of failure hung over this opportunity. I could wreck the first time I drove it and waste all the money I had spent to buy it. I told myself that I could never be good enough to compete in a race. I told myself I didn't have the knowledge it takes to make a car go fast. The fears were relentless, as they were trying to sabotage a dream I had carried since a young boy playing with my matchbox cars.

This would be one of the few times my fears did not win. I did buy the car and raced for three years. I never did win a race but will always cherish those Friday nights heading to the track.

But there were far too many other opportunities that my fears had ruined. I ponder sometimes, what would my life look like if I hadn't allowed my fears so much power?

As I realized the cost of this fear in my life, God began to help me understand failure through a researcher and a past president. I was walking on my treadmill one day and noticed a presentation on the television by a researcher named Dr. Brené Brown titled *Daring Greatly*. She was sharing some of her experiences in life of trying to dare greatly, and then reading negative comments toward her on social media. While struggling with these comments, she came across a speech by former President Theodore Roosevelt on failure and life. The speech went like this:

"It is not the critic who counts; not the man who points out how the strong stumbles, or where the doer of deeds could have done them better. The credit belongs to the man who is actually in the arena, whose face is marred by dust and sweat and blood; who strives valiantly; who errs, who comes short again and again, because there is no effort without error and shortcoming; but who does actually strive to do the deeds…who spends himself in a worthy cause…who at worst, if he fails, at least fails while daring greatly, so that his place shall never be with those cold and timid souls who neither know victory nor defeat."

After hearing that quote and listening to Dr. Brown share, God began to speak into my heart about failure. He helped me to grasp that failure should never determine my identity. He said my identity would always be that of His precious little boy whom He loves dearly and wants to walk daily with and show the fullness of life. Another words, He had already given me an identity. Then He said, "I will always love you!"

He also told me that in this life, I could not achieve perfection on my own. I needed to quit trying so hard to avoid failure. Instead, let Him continue the refining work that will give me a pure heart. It is not within my abilities to live a perfect life. Only through the work of the Holy Spirit will I move towards Godly perfection. Then He said, "I will always love you."

He continued by telling me that when I do fail, run to Him and not away from Him. Even David ran back to Him while writing the Psalms. Peter ran back to Him even after denying Him three times. That is why He calls David a man after His own heart and why Peter became the rock upon which He built His church. These two giants of the faith chose God over their failures. Once again, He said, "I will always love you."

Then I was left alone to chew on what He had just told me. How everything He said contradicted what I always believed about failure. How He uses failure in our lives to show others His love. That He gave me an identity and even in my brokenness, that identity does not change. It is not conditional. Finally, even in the midst of my failures He still loves me.

I continue to learn a lot about failure. I am beginning to understand how God has guided me to use my failures to help others. Failure is losing its power over me, and I let God teach me through it. And I know and believe that despite my failures, He will always love me.

Reflection Questions

1. What fears control your life?

2. Where do these fears come from? When did they begin?

3. How has living with these fears impacted your life?

Chapter 17

The Calling

It has been 20 years since I met and began my real journey with God. I believe my acceptance of Christ as my Savior and Baptism was a choice I truly made when I was 12. Then, I spent the next 30 years running or hiding from Him. Even though I went to church almost every week and read my Bible most days, I had an errant view of who God is. That is why I consider my journey with Him as really beginning 20 years ago at the age of 42. In those 20 years, He has been changing my heart and beliefs about Him. We have traveled to places I had only dreamed of going one day, and He has spoken through me in ways I thought impossible.

Along the way, God has led and introduced me to the career that has become my calling. It actually started in my 40s when I met Joe Donaldson. Joe and I were having lunch a while back, and I was sharing a thought that had entered my mind: "Within reason, having been retired for a few years

The Calling

now, and the daily responsibilities of raising a family mostly behind me, I could try any job I wanted to do." As I pondered that thought, it became frustrating, as nothing stood out to me as a feasible choice.

As Joe listened intently to my dilemma, he looked at me and responded, "Bob, you are already doing it." I had not realized it before because it was unlike any other job or career I had experienced, but he was right.

As a young person, I often thought I would go into the ministry in some way. I would always follow that thought with another: "I am so messed up, and I don't think God even loves me. There is no way He would want me in His ministry." Therefore, the idea of being in the ministry never made it beyond a thought. Yet, God has led me to be in ministry for 20+ years. I have no seminary degree or formal training. My only degree is in forestry, and it's an associate degree at that. Like most people God used in the Bible to show His love to the world, He rarely uses my strengths, but instead chooses to use my weaknesses — my struggles with sin. By now, you know I have plenty of those.

God knew I would struggle with thinking I was in the ministry, so He allowed it to begin slowly. He began by using Joe's ministry and inviting me to help him lead retreats. Each retreat, Joe would stretch me and help me to face a new fear. It actually took me three retreats before Joe was able to get me to share my talk by myself. A few years later, he would ask me why I always read my talk. I responded that I didn't want to forget anything, and reading helped me to focus. Joe affirmed to me that I knew my story better than anyone, and just sharing it from my heart would help more men to hear it.

God then led me into mentoring men at our church. Chris had told Tony, who oversaw our Men's Mentoring Program, that I would be a good candidate to become a mentor. Tony called me and invited me to come to his office and chat. As Tony explained that he was interested in me becoming a mentor, I quickly stopped him and asked, "Did Chris not tell you about me? I am a messed-up dude. I am sure there are other guys that would be a better fit."

To which Tony responded, "Bob, if you came in here telling me you had it all figured out, you would be no use to me. God uses broken people, and He wants to use you." Soon after, I began the three-and-a-half-month training to become a mentor.

God eventually led Joy and I into ministry together, as we began marriage mentoring. Today, you will find us teaching marriage classes and leading retreats. I guess it's time to acknowledge God is making ministers out of us, using our tongues to profess His great love, using our legs to let others know how much He pursues us, and using our story to show how much grace He has for His children.

A few years ago, Joe and I were talking over lunch about life. I shared with Joe the thoughts I was having about the three careers I have experienced in life — my air traffic control and woodworking careers, followed by a career in ministry. I said to Joe, "In my first two careers, I made decent money and had a consistent work life. This last career always costs me money, and I never know where I am going next! I would not have it any other way because this last career is by far the most challenging and fulfilling. There is no way I can do it on my own, and I think God likes that. And I know my wealth and knowledge are growing in other ways."

Even as God moves me through ministry and loving people, He continues to grow me, confront me, and love me. He is great at multitasking. Brennan Manning wrote in his

The Calling

book *The Ragamuffin Gospel: Good News for the Bedraggled, Beat-Up, and Burnt Out,* "God loves us as we are…not as we ought to be because we are never going to be as we ought to be." That quote has become very dear to me, for like Brennan, I have come to acknowledge that I will never be as I ought to be. At least not on this side of Heaven.

I also realized something different about this career in ministry God had led me into: My time is not my own, and I don't control what will happen from day to day. My job is to be in communion with the Holy Spirit and follow His lead.

While counseling with Chris, he began to see the rigidity in my life, and how full I kept my schedule. During one of our sessions, he became concerned about how strict my life had become. As we sat across from each other, Chris calmly said, "Bob, I think it would be good for you to one day get in your car and take a drive on Interstate 64."

I asked, "Where do you want me to go?"

Chris responded, "I don't know."

To which I asked, "What direction should I go?"

Chris quietly said, "I don't know."

Confused, I asked, "How far do you want me to go?"

Chris mumbled, "As far as you want to."

Becoming frustrated, I blurted out, "That's the dumbest thing I've ever heard."

Chris had made his point. How would I ever hear the Holy Spirit's guidance if I always had to be in control and live out a life planned completely? It took a while for it to sink in, but Joy and I began to take vacations, in just the way Chris was encouraging me during that session. Some of our most memorable times have been getting in a car or plane without a clue where our travels would take us or the people we would meet.

I know we all have responsibilities and things in life that are necessary for us to accomplish. I also know as I release my calendar to God more and focus on Him alone, He takes me on amazing journeys in life. I don't have to worry about what my destination is, which direction I should go, or how far it is going to be, because He is becoming my guide in life. And I am learning to allow Him to take care of my scheduling.

After 20 years of walking with Jesus and witnessing the miracles He has carried out in my life and others' lives, the draw of sin and ego remains. Lust can still try to rear its ugly head, and a critical spirit brought on by my very own ego constantly taunts me away from the peace of God. Even after all He has done for me, my fragile heart can have days when it still cries out, "God, do you really love and care about me?"

The apostle Paul writing to the Philippians in Chapter 3 about his journey of faith refers to this in verse 12: "Not that I have already obtained this or am already perfect, but I press on to make it my own, because Christ Jesus has made me his own."

So what do we do with the reality that we will never be perfect? That we will never be totally like Christ while on this earth? Do we give up or try harder?

The Calling

Paul continues his conversation in Philippians 3:14 when he says, "I press on toward the goal for the prize of the upward call of God in Christ Jesus."

At first reading, that sounds to me like I should try harder. Trying harder has only led me to more defeat, shame, and guilt. Worst of all, it created more distance between God and myself.

I was contemplating this idea of maturing in Christ and how that happens one day, and this little poem came out of my pen:

Will I ever be strong enough to run as Joseph did?
Or will I always want to stand on the balcony next to David?
And will I ever have the wisdom as Solomon had,
To know that my sin will never give me what I really want?

To be honest, that poem left me with a disheartening thought, as I feared the answers. After years of walking close with Jesus, my sinful nature is waiting around every corner. There is still sin in my heart that I was not aware of, tugging at me.

My pen had stopped writing too soon. There was more to the poem, and the Apostle Paul had already written it. In Romans 7, Paul shares his challenges with sin and concludes with verse 24, saying this: "Wretched man that I am! Who will deliver me from this body of death? Thanks be to God through Jesus Christ our Lord!"

That verse helped me to see there was an ending to my little poem that I needed to add, and it went like this:

On my own, the answer is grim.
But through the power of Jesus,
I will be strong enough to run like Joseph.
I will walk away from the balcony unlike David,
And I will know that sin will never fulfill me like the love of God as Solomon learned.

I began to embrace my brokenness. This phrase has caused some kickback from a few of my friends. The responses often include:

"Don't you want to be a better Christian?"

"Does that mean you are not trying to stop sinning?"

And "Sounds like cheap grace to me."

I understand their concerns for such a statement, and 25 years ago, it would have frightened me when it came out of my mouth. Today, however, it means something so different.

The first 42 years of my life were all about containing the broken pieces of Bob Head. I would often try to hide them in places where no one could see them, not realizing the spot they had vacated was still visible. I tried to locate pieces from another area of my life, thinking they might fill that gap and make me whole again. Other times, I would just run from the brokenness and numb myself so I did not have to see how broken my life had become. My attempts to reassemble the perfect vessel that in my mind God required for Him to love me always proved futile. As all this manipulation continued for years on end, my hope dwindled like a ship lost at sea. The sad reality began to set in: I was not capable of repairing and replacing all the broken pieces that made my very being.

The Calling

There is a centuries-old Japanese art form called Kintsugi. Kintsugi is the art of putting pieces of pottery back together using gold as an adhesive. Every break in the pottery is unique, and instead of repairing it to look flawless, the artist uses this technique to highlight the "scars" as a part of the design. The idea was built on embracing flaws and imperfections. As a result, the pottery becomes stronger and even more beautiful than before, as the gold outlines the broken areas. The value of the pottery also grows exponentially as it goes through this process.

With that in mind, here are some things I have learned about my brokenness.

First, God continually uses my brokenness, my sinfulness, to help others. I know I have already said this, but it was so important for me to learn that I feel the need to repeat it. That does not mean I try to be more broken. If I truly love God, it will break my heart when I stray from Him, which will cause me to run back to Him desiring to stray no more.

I really thought God would use my strengths when my journey with Him began. My woodworking skills to build things for church. My home-repair skills to help struggling widows. My nature photography skills to help others see His beautiful creation. While He certainly has used some of these things, by far my sexual addiction, my fear of failure, my fear of public speaking, and many more of my broken pieces are what He chooses to use the most. God used Moses's anger issues and lack of verbal skills and Peter's denial of Christ three times. There are many more stories that are similar in the Bible that reflect this.

Second, my brokenness brought me to a deeper relationship with God. When I tried to hide my brokenness, I also hid from God. When I embraced my brokenness and become vulnerable to Him, our relationship became much more intimate.

Third, the fact that no human being including myself can fix my brokenness has become a reality to me. It has to be in the skilled hands of the Creator who made me. The fact that my brokenness does not surprise God was an important revelation to me. He cares more about my broken heart than my behaviors. Yes, He knows my behaviors are sinful at times, and they are not good for me. He also knows there is a false belief in my heart that motivates those behaviors, and that false belief includes an inaccurate view of who He is, and that grieves him. Brennan Manning believes that when we arrive in Heaven, God will have only one question for us, which is, "Did you believe that I loved you?"

I want to live so my answer will be, "Yes Dad, I did!"

How has this answer become more real to me? By surrendering more and more. I am a selfish, egotistical person. Daily I must sit with God and surrender these characteristics to Him repeatedly. To be honest, some days are easier than others. As time passes, my surrendering to Him is becoming a new normal. My heart has to be willing to receive what He has for me. Growth can be painful, and yet it is an essential part of our journey with Him.

Finally, I must be intentional in my walk with God. It is very easy to become complacent with life and growth in Christ. If forward movement is not constant, stagnation occurs, which leads to death. Being intentional in my faith has changed what my life looks like. From the kinds of conversations I have, to the books I read and how I read them, to where my priorities are placed, to how I spend each day. God's ways are not the world's ways, and as we begin to walk with God, we begin to question much of what the world says. The things of this world are becoming less of a draw to me as I realize they only draw me away from Him.

I was talking to my friend Jerry recently. We were reminiscing about our faith journeys when Jerry looked at me and said, "Bob, I am glad you picked the right tree." I asked him what he meant by that statement, and he responded, "You didn't pick the oak tree to run your truck into and die. Instead you picked the tree that Christ died for you on, and you have life. I am glad for that."

I will always be thankful for that second tree and the man that died on it for you and me. I know there are more pieces for God to repair and more beauty for him to reveal. I also know I am in the hands of the best potter there is.

Thank you, DAD. I love you!

Reflection Questions

1. How has your view of God changed along your journey of faith?

2. In what areas of your life do you see God wanting to grow you right now?

3. Have you accepted your brokenness, or are you still trying to earn God's love? How is that working for you?

4. Do you believe your brokenness can bring you to a closer relationship with God? Why?

Words of Joy (Literally)

Written By: Joy Head, Bob Head's Wife

I have to admit feeling a bit overwhelmed. We have always shared "our story" with individuals, couples, and small groups, and on marriage retreats, but it's never been "made public." There are still friends and family unaware of the things you've read so far. They just know we're happy — not how we arrived at this wonderful place.

Oh my goodness, where do I start?! Bobby and I attended the same grade school, junior high, and high school. I had a crush on him in fifth grade; he was the captain of the safety patrol, after all. But we never met until he was away at college. I guess timing is everything. We dated for four years and were married on May 23, 1981.

We recently celebrated our 40th wedding anniversary. Miracles *still* happen, and we are living proof! Our daughter and son-in-law threw a surprise party for the special occasion. They really got us good! It was an awesome afternoon of laughter and sweet tears as we reflected with friends and family on the past 40 years. The theme of the party was "Better Together" (and I believe that!). There was a time, of course, when I wasn't so sure of that theme...22

years ago when I discovered the affair (after a good bit of snooping).

But God. (I love those two words!)

At that point, we had been married for 18 years. I would like to take some time to share a little bit about our journey from the perspective of the wife, and a few things we did that helped as we were trying to heal and protect our marriage. God placed wonderful people in our lives as we struggled through our recovery. Some we sought out (counselors, mentors, and class members at church), and some we prayed for (closer friendships, accountability groups, etc.). Some were a glorious surprise. All were a part of our healing. A few friends have been with us on most of our journey. Others have heard our story, when for similar reasons they needed some "hope with skin on" (the same kind of hope George and Cassie Soette, marriage mentors at our church, were for us!).

We were both Christians, but until this time, we never really understood what putting Christ in the center of our marriage looked like. It has made all the difference. We began reading a couple's devotional together before we went to sleep. I've never felt closer to Bobby as I do when we spend time together with the Lord. The Bible says in Ezekiel 36:26, "I will give you a new heart and put a new spirit in you; I will remove from you your heart of stone and give you a heart of flesh." God has done that for both of us.

We made a plan to date weekly, or at least every other week. This was a struggle for our daughter at first, since she had been the center of our world. But we were trying to save her world; she just didn't know it yet! We set out to reclaim places and things that we associated with a negative memory — whether it was a spot in our home, a restaurant, or an item

Words of Joy (Literally)

that was a "trigger" for some reason. Bobby even treated my best friend Mary and me to a girls' trip to Gatlinburg to reclaim our favorite vacation spot. It worked, and we've made years of happy memories as a family there since that time!

God also chose to challenge some of my personal flaws as we moved forward. Growing up with chronically ill parents, I struggled with a fear of abandonment (not *if* you will leave me, but *when*). I knew I kept people at an arm's distance, but I hadn't realized that Bobby's arm was out too, just for different reasons. God challenged me to believe He would never abandon me and that He was all I needed. One way He demonstrated this tangibly for us was when Bobby received a raise which paid the <u>exact</u> <u>amount</u> necessary for our counseling appointments.

I can also be passive at times. I love peace at all costs and always made excuses for everyone, even Bobby. Yet, in this case, God began to challenge me to care enough to confront my husband. Matthew 18:15 says, "If your brother sins against you, go and show him his fault, just between the two of you. If he listens to you, you have won your brother over." When I confronted Bobby about the affair, his first words were, "Who are you going to tell?" I could honestly say, "no one."

I am also a rule keeper (no wonder I had a crush on a safety patrol boy!) like the older brother in the story of the prodigal son in Luke 15, and the Pharisees throughout the Bible. I come from a couple of generations of grudge-holders — only to be challenged by a God who asked me to forgive Bobby and to pray for him. This was a tough one — and yet I felt like I was fighting for his soul. I really couldn't pray for him at the time as my husband, but I could pray for him as my brother in Christ. I could pray for a hedge of protection around him and for him to feel God's presence.

Bobby was Jen's daddy and also an idol that I had put up on a white horse, never feeling worthy of having him as a husband. I mean, the guy can do anything he tries, and can do it well; custom woodworker, Model A woody-wagon builder, award-winning photographer, house remodeler, guitar builder, and now add author! The affair (and all that went with it) kind of toppled him off that white horse back where he belonged. It put Bobby and me on even ground together at the foot of the cross, and put God back where He belonged, as my <u>only</u> God.

Bobby has mentioned the Faces of Christ retreat. Years ago, when I attended, my experience was equally good. Not a "mountaintop" experience like it is for some, but nevertheless an intimate time spent with God. I didn't gain, but instead lost something there — my anger toward my husband and God. Anger at Bobby for the affair, the pornography, and hurting me. Anger at God for allowing all this to happen. By realizing that God had gone through it with me every step of the way and that what Satan meant for evil, God was using for good, I could honestly say I was thankful that it happened. We could have kept plodding along, tolerating each other, without seeking the help we needed. Now I look back in amazement at the past 20 years and the differences in the life we have shared. We're having so much fun! We just enjoy being together!

One heart and life changed can impact so many others! What Bobby allowed God to do in him has influenced so many, starting with me. God used our weaknesses instead of our strengths. And I just love being "a ripple of God's love!" If He can save our marriage, He can save yours. If He can use us, He can use anybody!

Words of Joy (Literally)

This was all HARD work! It would have been easier to walk away, but I'm so glad that I didn't make that decision! We would've missed out on so much of life together — Jen's graduation, her wedding, our son-in-law's graduation from the police academy, the birth of our grandson Logan, both of our moms' illnesses and deaths, holidays, vacations, mentoring, and teaching. All of these experiences have been *Better* because we were *Together*!

We recently returned from out 40th anniversary trip out west. We saw some of God's greatest work! The Grand Canyon, Sedona's Red Rocks, The Painted Desert and The Petrified Forest; some of His amazing creations. I believe our marriage is one of these, too. It was fascinating to see flowers blooming on a prickly cactus or blossoms in barren desert areas where everything appeared dead, yet there it was: beautiful new life. I love symbolic pictures like that! And I love signs! My son-in-law Nate once said that I had so many signs, my house was starting to look like a Cracker Barrel (which is okay by me). Three of my favorite signs say:

"Contentment is not the fulfillment of what you want, but the realization of how much you already have."

"A perfect marriage is just two imperfect people who refuse to give up on each other."

And last but not least, "Never place a period where God has placed a comma." — Gracie Allen

To these, I say "AMEN!"

Joy Head

Jenny's Words

*Written by: Jenny McCoy,
Bob Head's Daughter*

To say that I am proud of my dad would be the understatement of the century. Sure, I'm proud of him for writing a book, but more so for the content in the book. He has humbly and vulnerably shared his mess with you, in hopes that you will see the hope, grace, and love that can only be found through a relationship with Christ.

If you are reading this, you already know his story. He asked me to write a few words about what it was like as a child growing up through his story. So here it goes (sorry, Dad). Growing up with him as a dad wasn't always easy. He tended to be short tempered, a workaholic, and would walk all over my mom. This led me to view my mom as very weak, and not until many years later would I realize just how strong she had been all those years! But for some reason, I was still a daddy's girl. If I wanted something, all I would have to do is call him "Daddy-roodles" and more than likely he would cave.

It is for this reason that I felt immense guilt when I suspected he had an affair. Sure, the evidence was there from the outside looking in as a young teenager. My parents didn't appear to have a healthy relationship. I would find porn on the computer when trying to play Oregon Trail (haha). I even read an email from someone that made me think an affair was going on. But I still felt guilt. How could my dad, who I held on a pedestal, be capable of that? How would he feel if he knew what I thought he was capable of?

Well, kids are more observant than you might think. I knew what was going on — at least I thought I knew. But it wouldn't be until college that I would get the courage to ask about it. By then, my dad had made a 180 turn thanks to lots of Christian counseling and allowing God to work in his heart. When I did finally bring it up, I felt a huge sense of relief. He humbly apologized for the impact his actions had on me throughout the years. We began having weekly lunch dates, we processed these things together, and I began to really value the wisdom he had as I was making my way into adulthood. You see, the Lord took what the enemy meant to destroy our family, and He used it for good.

Even as I saw my parents' relationship being healed, I was still leery of having one myself. What if I get in a relationship, and my partner cheats on me? I mean, my family doesn't have the best track record. This is something I still have to consciously work through with my husband. It has been difficult for me to be vulnerable and attached to him, with that fear of him hurting me and/or leaving me in the back of my head. Dads, your sin doesn't just affect you, and it doesn't just affect your spouse — it also affects your children, no matter their age.

    My husband and I have had some tough times of our own. Marriage is not really what either of us expected (is it ever?). But when we are having a tough time, it helps me to look at my parents' example. If they can make it through all they have endured, and come out stronger and more in love than ever, then surely we can make it through the bumps in the road!

    My parents have also always empowered me to share our family story whenever I feel led to do so. That's a pretty scary thing for them to be willing to do, but they acknowledge that it is my story too, that it can be therapeutic for me, and that I could encourage other families and children going through what we went through. I haven't shared that story a lot, but when I do, I don't feel embarrassment. I don't even care if people judge us. Instead, I am proud of us and grateful for our story. I am so proud of my parents, and their willingness to use their mess and turn it into a message of hope for others, and I want to impart that feeling of hope on others, too. It is not too late for you to have your own redemption story.

Sincerely,

The daughter of a ragamuffin

Suggested Resources

The Holy Bible:New International Version, Colorado Springs, CO, Biblica Inc. 1984

Brown, Dr Brene. *Daring Greatly:How the Courage to be Vulnerable Transforms the Way We Live, Love, Parent, and Lead,* New York City, NY, Avery Publishing, 2015

Dodd, Chip. *The Voice of the Heart,* Murfreesboro, TN: Sage Hill Resources, 2001

Larkin, Nate. *Samson and the Pirate Monks,* Nashville, TN: Thomas Nelson Inc., 2006

Manning, Brennan. *The Ragamuffin Gospel,* Sisters, MI: Multnomah Publishers, 1990

McGee, Robert S. *The Search for Significance,* Nashville, TN: Thomas Nelson, 1998

Ortberg, John. *The Me I Want to Be: Becoming God's Best Version Of You,* Grand Rapids, MI: Zondervan, 2010

Ortberg, John. *Soul Keeping:Caring for The Most Important Part of You,* Grand Rapids, MI: Zondervan, 2014

Rainey, Dennis and Barbara. *Moments Together for Couples,* Ventura, CA: Regal Books, 1995

https://www.thepotterswheel.org/retreats.html   *Faces of Christ Retreat*

https://samsonsociety.com/   *Samson Society Meetings*